Captain Black
True Stories of a Small Town Cop

Edward Black

As a Police Officer in the small town of Kaufman, Texas, just 30 miles Southeast of Dallas, Edward Black has seen his share of "Big-City" crime over his 20+ year career. He has also seen things that made him sit back and ask himself "How has this person lived so long?".

Starting out as a Reserve Officer and working his way up through the ranks to the position of Captain, he dedicated his life to protecting his community and battling the never-ending supply of stupidity that cops all over the world deal with on a daily basis.

Black tells it like it is and holds no punches as he takes his readers on a trip through some of the most memorable cases, and hilarious situations, of his career.

One of those cases was the most famous murder case in recent history. As a member of the team of law enforcement officers that investigated the horrifying murders of Kaufman County Assistant District Attorney Mark Hasse, and then the District Attorney himself, Mike McClelland, and his wife Cynthia, Black gives us a glimpse inside the Incident Command Post, and those first days of the investigation, as viewed from his unique perspective.

Captain Black:
True Stories of a Small Town Cop

Captain Black:
True Stories of a Small Town Cop

Edward Black

Edward Black

2017

Copyright © 2017 by Edward G. Black

All rights reserved. This book or any portion thereof may not be reproduced or used in any manner whatsoever without the express written permission of the publisher except for the use of brief quotations in a book review or scholarly journal.

First Printing: 2017
Revised: 2019

ISBN-13: 978-0-9997256-0-3

Edward Black
Sunnyvale, Texas 75182

Ordering Information:

Special discounts are available on quantity purchases by corporations, associations, educators, and others. For details, contact the publisher at the above listed address.

U.S. trade bookstores and wholesalers: Please contact Edward Black at egblackpublishing@gmail.com.

Dedication

To my babies
Chelsea, Reagan, and Garrett
If Daddy can write a book,
Imagine what you can do.

Table of Contents

Acknowledgements 9
Introduction 10
It's different now... 14
Documentation is no longer just a report........................... 16
"My" Kaufman Police Department..... 17
First Day On The Job... 19
The Old Lady with the Mouse in the Wall... 21
From One Old Lady To The Next... 23
I got your ass!.. 25
Hand me some cuffs & Possession is 9/10th's of the law... 29
The girl in the middle room 32
Thank God for the dog catcher!.. 35
Something is not right man... 37
I need you in route to an animal related call... 41
How pissed off can you get at 3 in the morning? 43
Where are your clothes man?!? 46
Death in the Garden Center.. 49
Finally Justice- A 22 Year Old Cold Case Solved 52
He may be small, but he's got Meth on his side!................ 58
The Bloody Van.. 61
Having A Gay Old Time! 63
Pumping Away at the Pump House! 65
Neither Snow nor Rain nor Heat nor Gloom of Night.... 68
I dropped my keys... 70

He's a friend of the family	73
The Story of Kelley Osgan	74
How to start a day…	78
Good Lord he's deformed!	79
Difficult Story #1. The first time I had to really fight for my life	81
6,208 days before I had to pull the trigger	88
Crazy-Ass Woman At Circle K	93
Mr. Bacon has been robbed again.	95
Largest drug find of my career	99
Difficult Story #2-The Murder Case of Kelley Osgan	102
The Standoff on Main Street	110
Difficult Story #3-The Hardest Story To Tell	115
Pit Bulls Suck!	119
If that's not a bag of dope I'll salute you!	122
Working the Hurricanes	125
PEARLAND & BEAUMONT, TEXAS	126
HOUMA, LOUISIANA	131
HOUSTON, TEXAS	132
The Kaufman County DA Murders….My Perspective	137
The Incident Command Post	141
The Nightmare Continues	144
The Prime Suspect	145
The Conviction	148
Afterthoughts	148

Aubrey Wright Hawkins 1971-2000..150

The Captain's Take on the State of Law Enforcement In 2017......
....154

Final Thoughts..159

Acknowledgements

I have kicked around the idea of writing a book for many years but never thought that I was intelligent, or educated enough to make the words say what I wanted them to say. So I started thinking about what I could write that might interest people, and what do I know enough about that I could pull it off without looking like a dummy.
It finally came to me that people are always asking me about my career and things that have happened during my time as a cop. Why not write about that? This book could never have been written if it weren't for many people whose contribution, in one way or another, allowed my dream to become a reality.

Above all else I want to thank the good Lord above for keeping me alive over the last 20-plus years. Only he and I know how close I've come to meeting him in person.
I want to thank my amazing, beautiful bride Leslie. Without you being my sounding board and taking care of me, I don't know where I'd be. I love you.
To my three beautiful children I want to say thank you for letting Daddy look at you and remember why I do this job. Daddy worships the air you breathe.
I want to thank my Mom, Charles, Kevin, and Tim for going easy on me when I wasn't able to make it to family functions because of the job.
To my "Work Family"; Robin, Joel, Lori Lynette, T. Bohn, Dian, Fletcher, Big Jim, Les, T. Black, Jason, Kandice, Sharna, Colter, Nick, Johnny, Connie, James Michael, John, Billy, and every other Officer that I have stood on the line with, Thank You for everything we've been through together, especially the laughs!
To the Police Chief's that I have served under I thank you for the opportunities and the lessons.
I especially want to thank Doug Barker. Life threw us a curve ball in the end, but for all of those hours spent together laughing and saving each other's asses, I thank you brother.

Introduction

Growing up, I always wanted to be the good guy. Whenever my friends and I would play cops and robbers, or space rangers, I was always on the side of right. The one that saved the day, the one that helped people.

I always wanted to be a Police Officer as far back as I can remember. Well, that's not entirely true, I wanted to be a Game Warden first but the college that they required put that goal well out of my reach. Not necessarily financially out of reach, but energy wise, it was WAY out of reach. I didn't want to work that hard at college. I did manage to get through one semester of "Introduction to Criminal Justice" at Trinity Valley Community College in Terrell, but I never could figure out how my knowing what happened in England in the early 1800's was going to help me be a good cop in 1990's Texas.

So I did my research and found out that I can attend the police academy at Eastfield College in Mesquite, Texas. At the time, I had a wife and baby girl to feed, so I attended evening classes five days a week and worked full time at the Pep Boys Distribution Center in Mesquite during the day. The academy was dry and mostly boring book work, but the war stories told by the instructors about their experiences as cops on the streets kept the fire inside me burning brightly.

I would be remiss if I didn't give some of the credit to my first wife Michelle for pushing me through the academy. There were times when I wanted to give up and quit. It was exhausting working all day and then going to school at night but she kept me focused on my goal and I thank her for that.

I completed the academy, passed the state test and was awarded a Basic Peace Officer license, which is quite hilarious because the last damn thing you have as a cop is peace. I went to work as a Reserve Officer (volunteer) for the City of Kaufman, Texas in 1996. I was hired on as a full-time Police Officer in 1998 and have spent my entire career in this little town. I went from a Reserve Officer, to a Full-Time Police Officer, to a Detective, to a Sergeant and then took a huge leap to Captain.

Being a Police Officer in a small town forces you to make a huge decision right at the beginning, before you do anything else. You see, every small town in the world is filled to the brink with the "P" word……….Politics. The most disgusting, and despicable, word in the English language. When you become a small town cop you must decide immediately if you are going to play along with the politics, where the law only applies to certain people, or if you are going to fight the small town establishment and enforce the law equally for the entire time you wear a badge………………… I chose the latter.

Something that has always fired me up is a person who thinks that they are somehow better than everybody else. You know them, they are the ones who will complain to the city council about how having cops working traffic is a waste of their tax dollars, yet they never seem to mention the 27 false alarms we have had to answer at their residence the last couple of months because they refuse to have the piece of shit alarm unit repaired.

I have seen people stand up and protest about how it would ruin the community to have an adult novelty store near the city "because people who shop at those places are low-lives and trash", when I know for a fact that the person doing the complaining has a bedroom full of sex toys and a sex-swing hanging from the ceiling! (Those alarm calls we answer when people accidentally rush out and leave their door open, can reveal a lot about them.) Being a cop in a small town teaches you real quick that everyone, *and I mean EVERYONE*, has at least one skeleton in their closet.

When you are training to become a Police Officer, they don't explain to you that you are not just putting on the "police" hat, you are putting on a whole shit-load of different hats! When you pin that badge to your shirt you become a Cop, Marriage Counselor, Financial Advisor, Big Brother, Father Figure, Handyman, Race Car Driver, Stunt Car Driver, Cowboy, Chef, Taxi Driver, Caretaker, Delivery Man, Doctor, Game Warden,

Firearms Expert, Psychic, Referee, Messenger, Fireman, Mechanic, Social Worker, Translator, Electrician, and many, many more. Sometimes you are forced to be judge, jury, and even executioner (of injured animals, not humans for those of you that may be a little confused).

The most important thing you will do, aside from staying alive, is learning how to understand the many different types of people that you will be interacting with, and how to deal with each type of person in a different, and appropriate manner. What may be perfectly acceptable to one person is often not tolerated by the next. Some words are fine with some people, and offensive to others. One example is the word "Mexican". Some people take great pride (rightfully so) in calling themselves, and being called a Mexican, while others will jump down your throat and tell you that they are "Hispanic, NOT Mexican!" even if they are from Mexico. That's just the way it is.

When all is said and done though, when you get through the cultural, societal, and racial differences, there are only two kinds of people. Oh sure, some people have a lot more money than others, or a bigger house, or nicer cars, but when it gets down to the nut-cuttin, you are either a good person or a bad one. For an officer of the law, the real challenge comes in sorting out who's who.

Another thing you have to figure out quickly is how to stay alive. Throughout the last 20 years, I have come close to dying more times than I can count. A couple of times I've come just about as close as you can come to death and still walk away. I will tell you about some of those events in this book, along with some of the hilarious, crazy-ass experiences that go along with being a small town cop.

My hope, more than anything else, is that I make you laugh, and at the same time help you better understand what it's really like to wear a badge. I also want to try to open myself up beyond my comfort zone and give you a glimpse at some of the messed-up crap that I've kept to myself for a long time.

If you are easily offended, step back, put the book down, and walk away! If you don't take yourself too seriously, can laugh at a joke, and want to read about what goes on in Kaufman, Texas and small towns everywhere.....turn the page and enjoy.

Captain Edward Black

It's different now......

Being a Police Officer in 2017 is a world away from being one in 1998 when I began my career in Kaufman, Texas, (Pop 7400 according to the government, a lot more in reality) a small town about 30 miles southeast of Dallas for all you non-locals. Back then, people respected the police. They looked up to police officers and appreciated the job we did. Parents raised their kids to look to the police when they were lost or needed help. Today they teach them how to flip us off before they even begin kindergarten. They teach them to fear us, they tell them that *we* are the bad guys, and they teach them their most important life-lesson of all, "*NEVER talk to the cops, and never snitch*".

As I write this book, I am amazed at how we, as a society, have allowed ourselves to fall this far. I listen to all of the people out there on television who are supposed to be "experts" telling us that the reason we don't respect one another is because of all the chemicals in our food, or the atmosphere is warming up......BULLSHIT! I have paid attention over the last 20 years to the changes in the way people think, the way they accept and deny responsibility, and I believe I know why we are in the shape we are in. (Just hear me out and stop rolling your eyes)

The reason there is no longer any respect among people in America comes down to one thing.........*babies started having babies.*

That's right, 13 and 14 year old children started having children. Girls (and of course boys) started having sex at younger ages and suddenly we have 26 year old grandparents. These girls were not ready to be parents, of course, and they have no intentions of giving up their carefree way of life just yet. So what happened? The teenagers that suddenly have real life babies to take care of decide that, instead of taking responsibility as parents and staying home on Friday and Saturday nights, they would just take their babies along with them while they went out and partied.

Now, all of the sudden, her friends think it's cool that she is getting all of the attention because she has a baby, so they go out and get pregnant. The result of this new "fad" is that we now have young women dragging babies along with them while they get drunk, smoke dope, get tattoos all over their necks, and act like trash. The impressionable little minds soak all of this up, thinking it is the way they are supposed to behave, and the fuse is lit.

But the gravy on the biscuit, is that these babies are raised by immature, selfish, juvenile parents who pound it into their head that the only thing that's important is "*ME ME ME*". *To hell with everyone else, all I care about is what benefits me, and only me, right now!* They were taught that they should do whatever they want to do, when they want to do it, and worry about tomorrow, tomorrow. They were taught to spend every penny they have to buy that new phone, and worry about your bills, rent, and diapers later. Fast forward to 2017 and the fuse has burned down causing an explosion of a generation that is the epitome of selfishness.

Most of the younger people of today have no compassion for one another. These young man and women have been raised in a society that drenches them in violence day after day, hour after hour. Video games where they learn the art of decapitating a human being, television shows that empower heartless killers, and music that preaches to them that it's okay to "*Kill a muthafuckin cop*" are what they ingest on a daily basis, beginning the day they are born.

This generation that we call the "millennials" are the first generation to ever believe that it is more important to video record the old lady getting the hell beat out of her, instead of stopping the abuse, or even calling for help. They believe that taking a picture of the man lying on the ground bleeding, and posting it on social media, is far more important than giving their fellow human being first-aid. They also believe whole-heartedly that their rights vastly outweigh anyone else's.

I'm not a genius by any stretch of the imagination, but I am smart enough to know that if you beat on a kid every day of his life, he's going to believe that he is supposed to be beaten on. I'm also smart enough to know that if your parents smoke and drink, then you are more likely to smoke and drink. It's simply human nature. When a child is raised by parents that wouldn't know respect if it came in a bottle, how is that child supposed to learn how to respect others? That is what I believe, if you don't believe the same way, that's perfectly fine with me. We can still be friends.

Documentation is no longer just a report.

So yes, being a cop today is a lot different, and more difficult, than it used to be. There used to be a time when a law enforcement officer's testimony in court actually carried some weight, but not anymore. If it isn't recorded in crystal clear video that you can show a jury, then you can pretty much forget that case ever going to trial. And it had better be good video. If you can't see the dimples on a gnat's ass, don't even bother.

Most officers of today wear body cameras on their uniforms. They have cameras in their patrol vehicles, cameras on their guns, cameras on their sunglasses, and cameras on their Tasers. Hell, they would make us put them on our shoes if they weren't scare that some of us would be looking up women's dresses with them! We are quickly approaching the time when a crime will only be prosecuted if the entire offense is recorded on video.

The reason for all of this is simple; bad cops. There are many bad cops out there, just like there are many bad firefighters, doctors, and teachers out there. The only difference though, is if a single cop, in a back alley, in a small town in California is caught beating on someone, then ALL cops everywhere are doing it! We are the only profession where every single member is judged by the actions of one. This of course is just my opinion, but there has been no one yet that has proven to me that it's not a justifiable statement.

What people do not understand, even in Kaufman, Texas, is that good law enforcement officers hate a bad cop. We despise them.

They go against everything that a good cop believes in and they tear down, in an instant, the good relationships with the community that take us months or years to build. Our small department is not immune from bad cops either. We have had to deal with the issue of an officer that shouldn't be wearing a badge, just like a lot of departments do. Most of the time we handled the problem very well, sometimes, we flat-ass blew it.

"My" Kaufman Police Department...

The reason I say "My" Kaufman Police Department is because I am strictly speaking for myself in this book. The words and thoughts expressed are mine and mine alone. Neither the City of Kaufman, nor the Kaufman Police Department has anything to do with this little project of mine in any way. As they say....The views expressed herein are mine, and are not those of the City of Kaufman, or the Kaufman Police Department.

I also say that because I will be telling MY stories, from MY perspective, with MY words, and MY opinions, from MY memories. There are certain people that will get offended or pissed off about some things that I am going to say in these stories, and that's okay, but everything that I say will be said the way it happened from my recollection. I don't plan on purposely kicking anyone under the bus, or embarrassing anyone, but if I'm going to write a book, I've got to tell the bad with the good.

Like any workplace, there have been good times, and there have been horrible times. For the first 12 years of my career the Police Department was the stepchild of the city. We were an unwanted necessity, and the city leaders up front never let us forget it either.

One example is when the Lieutenant, I, and a couple of other officers were outside with the hood up on one of the squad cars that was giving us problems for the umpteenth time. (The city didn't believe in buying new cars for the police department until we completely ran out of duct tape and bailing wire)

The Finance Director of the city walks by and decides to give us her unsolicited opinion. She asked us what was wrong and the Lieutenant told her that the car was just worn out because it had over 100,000 miles on it. She then stated *"well my van over there has 112,000 miles on it and it still runs great because I've taken good care of it"*. The Lieutenant turned around and said to her *"well exactly how many 100 mph pursuits have you been in in that van, huh?"*

Another example, and this one is my favorite, is the time a past City Manager told the Chief of Police that he didn't like the Police Officers wearing sunglasses because it made them look too militant and we intimidate the citizens. If I'm lying, I'm dying!

That was the mentality of city hall back then. They had no fucking clue about law enforcement or what it involved, yet they had full control over the police department and our budget. That's a dangerous combination that has resulted in many lawsuits around the country.

Over the years things have improved quite a bit, but there is still a long way to go to get to where we need to be. The leadership at city hall has improved dramatically, but there are other areas that need a lot of work. (That's a topic for another book)

Getting older also makes being a cop a lot harder than it used to be. One day you are out there chasing bad guys, feeling like a superhero, and the next day just putting on your duty-belt is like fighting a 10 foot python. Getting older also means you have to do things that you never, ever, thought you would be doing. I learned this the day my doctor walked in the exam room pulling on a glove telling me to drop my pants and bend over the table........Huh? The man had giant, swollen, arthritic knuckles and he violated me before I could even get ready! The Prostate is an evil organ.

From pinning on that first badge to pinning on Captain's bars seems like no time at all. Reflecting back on it today though, I can see it has been one long ass journey!

First Day on the Job...

It was my very first day on the job as a real-life, gun-totin, badge wearing Police Officer. I was assigned to ride in a patrol vehicle with a day-shift officer for a couple of hours and then hang over and ride with a night shift officer for a while. I was in the car for two hours when I was in my very first pursuit.......*two hours!* We were attempting to make a traffic stop on an old Chevrolet pickup that had three men in it. As soon as we turned on the red and blues they took off like a teenager caught in his girlfriend's bedroom in the middle of the night!

We chased them down Mulberry Street, up Dallas Street, across Grove Street and then they tried to cut through a ditch to lose us but we were right on their bumper! The old Chevy got stuck and we lock up the brakes and slid to a stop right behind them. I bailed out of the car and stand there like a dumbass looking at the guys in the truck. I look over at my training officer and he has his gun pointed at the truck. *Damn!* So I unholster my weapon and stand there shaking like I'm having an epileptic seizure. I'm thinking to myself, *"Shit, did I even load this damn thing? Do they have a weapon that I can't see? If I have to shoot, which one do I shoot first? I feel a draft, are my pants unzipped, because if I get shot I damned sure don't want my fly to be open when everybody looks at me, hell this is my first day for God's sake!!"*

Thank goodness my training officer took charge of the situation and directed me on what to do and everything turned out good. Bad guys went to jail and I got in the car with my night shift trainer for a few hours. There couldn't be any more excitement on this day..........right?

My heartbeat had finally started slowing down from the pursuit and arrest when we were driving up East First North Street, (yes, that's the real name of this street). East First North Street is in an area called "The Hill" and it was your typical drug infested high crime area at that time. Lined with run down, plank-board houses on each side and a funeral home sitting right smack dab in the middle of the block, it was a continuous block party at all hours of the day and night.

We were driving up the street and spot a large group of people standing in the road, drinking their beer and smoking who knows what. We pass the group and the other officer asks me "Did you see the guy in the red shirt? We have a warrant for his arrest". He circles the block and pulls over to the side of the road, about 30 yards from the crowd, and we get out. The training officer calls out "*hey cornbread, come here*". The guy in the red shirt then walks over to us. The training officer tells him that he has a warrant and he is under arrest so I put my handcuffs on him.

He starts raising hell saying that he is not Cornbread and that he is promptly going to sue our asses for false arrest. After about 10 minutes of checking into his claims it turns out that he really isn't Cornbread. His name is June bug. We release the guy and he walks off cussing us like we kicked his dog and we drive back to the station. We walk into the station and there stands June bug! He had beaten us back to the station to file a complaint against us! My first day and I'm getting a complaint filed against me, are you freakin kidding me!?" Well the training officer goes and finds a picture of Cornbread and brings it out and shows it to the Chief and June bug. They could be twins. Then the Chief asks June bug, "Why did you answer to the name Cornbread when the officers called you over to their car?" His answer...."*Sometimes I go by cornbread*". I decided that I'd had enough for my first day and took my butt to the house!

The Old Lady with the Mouse in the Wall...

I was working the night shift along with my sergeant and another officer. It had been a pretty quiet night up until midnight. That's when I got the call to respond to Wayne Street for an "Assist a Citizen" call. Now, we all hated "Assist a Citizen" calls because they could be anything from a barking dog to a psychotic clown in the attic, you just never knew.

I walk up to the house and notice that there doesn't appear to be any lights on inside. I knock on the door and after a minute or so a hunched over little old lady who appeared to be about 97 years old answered the door. As I had summarized, there were no lights on inside the residence except for one small lamp that I could see down the entryway into the living room area. I introduce myself and she looks me in the eye and says *"follow me"*.

I said "ma'am can I ask what the problem is before we go inside?" But she keeps walking and repeats her earlier command, *"Follow me"*. I ease my way down a long hallway and into the living room area and she walks across the room and turns around. *"Smell that?"* Still a little uneasy, I asked "smell what ma'am"? So she points her long bony finger towards a wall and says *"there's a dead mouse in that wall"*. I stood there for a second trying to make sure I had heard her correctly, and then I said in my best professional police officer voice *"Ma'am?"*

She again points at the wall and says *"there is a dead mouse in that wall; I can smell him from my bedroom! I want you to take this sledgehammer and knock a hole in the wall and get him out. He stinks!"* I then realize that she had walked over by a door and was trying to drag a 20 pound sledgehammer toward me. She couldn't lift it. I said *"ma'am where did you get that sledgehammer?"* And she promptly informs me that it doesn't matter where she got that sledgehammer and for me to get busy with it!

Now keep in mind that it is after midnight, in a dark house, with a woman that's older than retail shopping is and she wants me to knock a hole in her wall to get out a dead mouse, that she says she can smell from her bedroom! I tried to explain to her that I simply couldn't knock a hole in her wall and that she should call an exterminator or maybe a family member to help her. I said *"Ma'am I don't smell anything, are you sure there is a dead mouse in your wall?"* Well, that was a mistake!

"Are you telling me that I don't know what I smell young man? I have been smelling dead critters since before you were even born, I know what I smell! I may be old but my nose still works, now you catch hold of that sledge and get to work! I pay my taxes!" Right about then, I hear a knock at the door. I excuse myself, as she continues her rant, and I walk to the door. I open the door and there stands my Sergeant. He asks *"hey, what's going on?"* I said *"she wants to speak to my supervisor, I'll catch ya later."* I then make a prompt exit and hit the road as fast as I can!

I caught all of the shit calls for a few days but it was well worth it. And it wasn't the last time I would use the "she wants to speak to my supervisor" bit either!

From One Old Lady to the Next

Anyone who is familiar with Kaufman, Texas knows about "The Curve". We have this huge curve in the highway where Highway 175 and Highway 243 meet. The road not only curved, but it dropped down a hill as well. This location was notorious for being dangerous in wet weather. And I don't mean normal "dangerous in wet weather" either, I mean if someone spit on the road, there was a crash!

We used to go out when the rain started and video record crashes at the curve while they happened. I would go out to the service road, turn on the video camera and wait. I wouldn't have to sit there long. You could almost set your watch by it. Whenever it started raining, we would automatically head to the curve. It took years for the state to finally decide that enough carnage had occurred to justify going out there and making the road safe.

One day it had been raining off and on for hours and I was dispatched to a crash out there. When I arrived on scene I observed a car, facing the wrong direction, up against the guardrail at the bottom of the curve. I parked my car up the road about seventy-five yards and walked down, keeping a very close eye out behind me, just waiting for the next car to come around and lose control.

I made my way down to the car and found an 83 year old woman trying to climb over to the passenger side, because the driver's door was up against the guardrail and she couldn't open it. Now, I have had a lot of experience working accidents in the curve, and I knew it was just a matter of time before someone comes along, loses control and possibly takes out this car. I had already heard several cars skidding their tires on the wet pavement as they attempted to slow down when they rounded the curve and spotted us. I knew I had to get her out of there and off of the highway fast.

I got half-way inside the vehicle and manage to practically lift her over the center console and hauled her out of the car. I got her to her feet and while she is trying to catch her breath she was trying to talk to me, but I interrupted her and tried to explain to her that we had to get off of that highway as fast as possible. Now, where we were, there was a guardrail that's about 2 feet tall and she was not going to be able to easily get over this thing. As I am attempting to walk her to the end of the guardrail, I heard it. The unmistakable sound of tires skidding sideways on wet asphalt!

I glanced up to see a U-Haul box truck sliding straight at us. It has already passed my patrol car and was almost on top of us. We were still 30 or 40 feet from the end of the guardrail and there was no way she was going to be able to jump over it by herself. I grabbed her in a bear hug and dove over the guardrail with her in my arms. Just as we hit the ground, the truck slammed into the guardrail and then her car and both vehicles went sliding and grinding along the guardrail for about 60 feet before coming to a stop.

When I came to my senses, panic instantly overwhelmed me because I think that I have killed this poor old lady by grabbing her, diving over the guardrail, and landing on top of her! I jumped up and grabbed her arms, "*Ma'am can you hear me? Can you talk to me, breathe! Breathe! Can you hear me!?!*" She then opens her eyes, looks at me, smiles and says "*Young man I haven't had a thrill like that in 40 years!*" If I'm lying I'm dying.

She brought me some home-made chocolate chip cookies to the police department about a week later. You can't make this stuff up!

I got your ass!

One of my most proud accomplishments was getting a pedophile off the streets of Kaufman and into a jail cell where he belonged. This is how it happened.

The front door of the police department opened as I was standing in the dispatch area and I knew immediately that whatever this woman wanted to talk about, she meant business. She looked passed the dispatcher at me and said "*I want to talk to you!*" I had never before seen this woman, so as I walked out to the lobby area I was trying to think of who I had pissed off recently. But it had been a good couple of weeks and I didn't remember anyone that stood out with their pissiness.

I opened the lobby door and said "*Yes ma'am, what can I do for you?*" Then she started crying! She told me that her little girl had come home from school and said something to the effect of "Mommy, that man showed me his thing again". She asked her daughter what she was talking about and the child began telling her about a man in a White pickup truck that would drive by her and her friends while they were walking home from school and lift himself up in the truck to show them his "thingy".

I managed to calm the woman down and got her to tell me all of the specifics. We set her daughter up to be interviewed by a special child advocate, but that wasn't going to happen for a few days. I drove around the schools for the rest of the day looking for a White pickup driven by a man, (that's all we knew at that point) without any luck.

A few days later, another woman brought her daughter in to file a report. The little girl told us that an older, heavy set, white man drove by her and her friends the day before, while they were walking home from the same school as the other child, and when he passed them, he rose up and showed them his penis. But there was one key difference; he was driving a Blue Ford Mustang, not a White truck.

I finished my report and went to my Sergeant. "I want to try to catch this guy and the best way to do that is to be in the area in a regular car, not a marked patrol car". He said "we don't have any regular cars to use" and before he could say anything else I volunteered to use my personal car. I told him if he would cover the streets, I would catch this guy. He hesitantly agreed (mainly because he was the laziest damn cop on earth and there was a risk that he might have to actually take a call while I was trying to catch this prick) and I took off my uniform shirt, got in my car and went to get into place to wait.

I drove over to Nash Intermediate School on South Houston Street and parked in the parking lot of the school administration building, which was right next to the school. I was either looking for a White pickup truck or a Blue Mustang, but either way, I was looking for an older white male. To my amazement, I didn't have to wait long.

From where I was parked I could see straight down West Second Street. The second little girl had told us that she and her friends were on that street when the man had shown them his "thingy". I hadn't sat there more than 10 minutes when I see an older model, white colored truck coming up West Second Street toward me. As he approached the stop sign I saw that the driver was an older looking white male, with white hair, just as the little girls had described. He stopped at the intersection and looked around for just a few moments longer than he should have in my book, so I decided to follow him.

He turned right on Houston Street, drove a short distance, turned right onto Seago Street, then turned right again on South Jefferson Street. *He was circling the block!* He went down to West Second Street and turned right, headed straight back the way he had come when I first spotted him. THEN HE DID IT!!! As he passed a group of 5 or 6 little girls who were walking on the side of the road, he lifted himself up as far as he could in the truck and was staring at the kids. *You sorry pedophile bastard!*

I got on the radio "9117 to all units, I GOT HIM! He just did it right in front of me! Get me a marked unit over here to stop this guy!" I continued following this perverted piece of shit as he was making the exact same trip around the area again. One of the Criminal Investigators who had red and blues in her car managed to catch up to us and get the truck stopped. I ran up to the truck, almost pushing the Detective out of the way and told him *"I GOT YOUR ASS you piece of shit!"* (We didn't record everything back then so if you were a piece of shit, sometimes you got told you were a piece of shit)

After I regained my professionalism, we got him out of the truck. He was wearing a tank-top and a pair of giant shorts that could have fit a 2 year old elephant, and no shoes. It was the perfect outfit for him to be able to pull his shorts down and yank out his mighty midget to flash little kids.

We identified him but had to let him go for the time being, because we needed an arrest warrant to solidify the case. However, before we let him leave, he agreed to come to the station to be photographed, (you know, because he is a dumbass) and we then used his picture to build a photo lineup. Later that day we showed the photo lineup to the little girls and they both picked him out immediately! Kids are AWESOME witnesses, they never forget anything!

The next morning, the Detective and I went to this hell-bound child molester's house and I had the pleasure of arresting him right in front of his wife. But the excitement of getting this sick prick off the streets was short lived. You see, unbeknownst to me, this pedophile was a friend of the Kaufman County Sheriff that held office at the time (early 2000's), and he was quietly released after spending a whopping 45 minutes in jail.

I had put everything I had into getting this man arrested, off the streets and away from those children and the highest law enforcement officer in the county lets him walk out the back door in less than an hour. This was my first lesson in Kaufman County politics, but it was far from the last. The "good ole boy" system was alive and well in Kaufman County!

Well, the bastard's high ranking buddy couldn't protect him from the rest of the judicial system for long. He was convicted and sentenced to several years in prison. It was nowhere near enough time, but at least we got him away from the community's kids. His wife, who had cussed me out when I arrested him that morning, later divorced him because he got caught in a public bathroom stall in Houston shoving a carrot in some guys poop chute or something like that.

Hand me some cuffs & Possession is 9/10th's of the law...

This was one of those nights that you just love being a cop! I and my best friend Doug were working together one night covering the night shift. We were both Criminal Investigators at the time, however, for one reason or other both of the regular night shift patrol officers needed to be off and me and Doug loved to get out of the office to play every once-in-awhile so we volunteered to work for them.

Let me start by saying that this two-day shift ended up with an article being written about us in the local newspaper, that's how much fun it was!

The first night started out with me spotting a car with one of the small, rear "vent" windows broken out. This is a good sign when looking for stolen vehicles. As I turned around the driver took off and the chase was on. I notified dispatch that I was in pursuit and began tailing the car all through a neighborhood that we called "New Town". I could see that there were 4 or 5 people in the car, and I was hoping they wouldn't all bail out before I could get some help close to me.

The driver made a mistake and turned into an apartment complex where a truck parked across the road blocked them in, with me right behind them. I yelled at the man who was standing next to his truck to get the hell away from there. To my relief, he did just as I asked. I think the old gentleman hurdled a dumpster trying to get out of there.

Also to my relief, nobody bailed out of the car! They all sat there long enough for me to get out of my squad and get them at gunpoint. When Doug arrived soon after, we removed the driver from the vehicle first. As he got out of the car I immediately recognized him as a local doper and thief that I had arrested several times before. I also knew that he was a convicted felon and was not afraid to fight the police.

We removed the suspects from the vehicle one at a time and put them face down on the pavement. I placed the first two suspects into custody using my handcuffs. When I went to arrest the third suspect I asked my buddy for his handcuffs. He looks at me real funny and says "wait a second" and walks to his car! Here I am with five suspects on the ground, trying to handcuff one of them, keep an eye on the other two that aren't handcuffed yet, and he tells me to wait a second?? It seems that my partner, who by the way is a great cop, had left his handcuffs at the police department. So here we sit, needing three pairs of handcuffs and having none.

At about this time, dispatch advises me that the car is stolen out of Dallas. I did the only thing that I could do and got on the radio and asked if there were any officers in the area that could bring me some handcuffs. After about five minutes goes by, my friend Big Jim, who is the Animal Control Officer, shows up with an arm load of handcuffs.

So as we cuffed up the last of the suspects, I was messing around with the driver of the stolen car and asking him "what kind of cop shows up at a bust with no handcuffs?" He really didn't know what to say so after I had thoroughly embarrassed my co-worker, I let it go. Shit happens.

We booked this group of fine citizens into jail for stealing the car, possession of drugs, and a gun I found in the front seat and then hit the streets again. We both decided to drive out to a piece of property that the city owned that was about 2 miles outside the actual city limits that went down to a huge lake. People liked to go out there and use drugs, have sex, and do who knows what else. I had made many arrests out there while I worked the streets. We got to the dirt road that goes back down to the lake and before we drove down in there we blacked out and drove by the light of the moon. We eased down the road in order to sneak up on anyone that may be out there and as we reach the main area near the water, I see a faint light coming from inside a car. We soon learned why the light was so faint and hard to see!

Doug and I parked and stealthily walked up to the car. There were three teenagers in the car, a girl and two guys, and they were smoking enough weed to fog up a magic show in Vegas! The smoke was so thick in the small car that we could barely make out what they were doing. I looked at my buddy Doug and as we both smiled, I tapped on the window.

It was hilarious watching them all try to stash their dope with cops standing on each side of the car. The brain surgeon in the backseat had stuffed a lit joint under his coat and it started to flame up. I was laughing my ass off. I told Doug to get the driver out first and as he opened the door, the smoke came out of the car and into the spotlight beams from our squad cars and it looked exactly like a Cheech and Chong movie! Doug looked over at me and had a look on his face like he was having a flashback to high school!

We cuffed them up (Doug had brought his cuffs this time) and collected all of their Marijuana. We made them stand at the rear of their car as we both got back in our cars to check them through dispatch and to warm up because it was cold standing out there with that wind coming off of the lake.

As I am sitting there waiting for my returns to come back, I looked up and could not believe my eyes....the little douche bag that I had removed from the back seat was wearing a t-shirt with the phrase "Possession is 9/10th's of the law"!! I called Doug on the radio and said *"Read his shirt!"* He got out of his car, ran over to the turd and was dancing around in front of him, laughing his ass off and asking the kid *"how stupid do you feel right now dumbass?!?"*.

We kept that kids' booking photo for years and laughed about it every time we saw it. That same kid was arrested several times after that and every time my partner would see him he would yell at the top of his lungs *"Possession is 9/10th's of the law!!! How the hell are you?"*

We ended up making 12 arrests in those two days. The local paper *The Kaufman Herald,* wrote an article about how Doug and I cleaned up the streets that weekend. Of course we caught hell from all of the other officers, but it was worth it. Thinking about that weekend makes me miss the streets again!

The girl in the middle room

It was the middle of summer and it was hot as usual. I was doing my best not to be out in the heat more than I had to and was hoping for an easy day....yeah right. I received a call regarding a "Welfare Concern" on a quiet street in town and headed that way.

When I arrived at the residence, a little frame house with a carport attached, I met with a couple of people who told me that their friend, Miranda, had not been heard from in 2 days. Her truck was parked under the carport, the doors were locked, all of the windows on the house were locked tight with the screens screwed into the house, and the blinds were drawn. Looking through the small window on the front door, I could see a purse and a pair of tennis shoes.

Her friends told me that Miranda never went anywhere without her purse, or without taking her truck, she always wanted to drive wherever they went. I knocked on the front door, the back door, and every window on the house, but there was no answer. I asked if she had family that may have picked her up or if maybe she had been dating someone that she may be with? The answer was always *"absolutely not, she is in that house!"*

The friends told me that they had been in contact with everyone they knew; including her family and nobody had heard or seen her in 2 days. I was beginning to get concerned that we were going to find a dead body once we got inside the house.

I called my Lieutenant and asked for assistance. He arrived a short time later with my shift partner. We again went to every door and window and performed the loud "police knock" but still no answer. The decision was made to put me through the kitchen window (I was the youngest and had less seniority than anyone else, so I drew the short straw).

We unscrewed the window screen over the small (and very high) window and they lifted me up enough for me to grab the window sill and pull myself through. As you can imagine, climbing through that small kitchen window with 30 pounds of gear strapped around me, I wasn't very subtle or sneaky about it! I knocked a drinking glass off of the counter and it broke into dozens of pieces while also announcing my presence to anyone who might be in the house.

I finally made it to my feet and took a second to gather myself and draw my weapon. The house was immaculate. The glass that I had broken was the single thing in the entire house that was out of place. There were no lights on, no television or computer on. It was dead silent. The only good thing was I didn't smell anything!

I slowly made my way around the kitchen into the living room where I could see the front door. To my left was a hallway with two doors on each side, all of them closed. The floors were all hardwood so every step I took made noise. I crept over to the front door and unlocked it. One thing that immediately caught my eye was that the chain had been latched; meaning whoever locked the door did it from the inside.

Once I opened the door, the Lieutenant and I started easing our way down the hallway, using signals so we didn't have to speak. I reached the first door, which was on the left side of the hallway. I slowly opened the door not knowing what the hell to expect. Bathroom, it was clear. As the Lieutenant approached the first door on the right side of the hallway, I eased up toward the next door on my side.

Suddenly I hear my Lieutenant......"*psst*". I turned around and he pointed with slow motions into the room where he was standing. I crossed over and eased back to the door and peaked around the corner. The room was stacked from floor to ceiling with boxes, with only a small walkway past them to the closet. There she sat. A chill went down my spine like you would not believe.

She was sitting there in the floor cross-legged, staring into the closet. She never made a sound. She was not injured, there were no signs of drugs or alcohol anywhere in the house, and she had to have known we were in the house. *What the hell!?*

My Lieutenant started speaking to her very softly, it was obvious she was in some kind of shock or depressed state, and we wanted to be as gentle as we possibly could. I made my way back outside the residence in the hopes of not scaring her by two of us standing there looking at her. As I walked outside the house her friends came rushing at me wanting to know if she was dead.

"*No she is not dead. She is in there, but there is something wrong with her and we do not know what it is yet*". I called her pastor, who she was close friends with, and a medical team to stand by. We still had no idea what was going on with Miranda yet and we wanted to be prepared for anything.

It took the Lieutenant 45 minutes just to get her to respond to him and agree to walk to the couch in the living room. At that point, her pastor and the medical team took over.

Miranda had fallen into a deep state of depression. She withdrew from everyone and everything, in her mind, all at once. This is unusual, but it does happen. We spent a couple of hours with her that day and I was glad to learn later on that she had made a great recovery with the help of her support system.

If you or your loved one suffers from depression of any kind, or have thoughts of harming yourself, please talk to someone. There is help out there.

Thank God for the dog catcher!

I was working the street and running traffic out on Highway 175 one afternoon. I stopped a 4-door Chevrolet pickup for swerving in and out of his lane. The driver didn't stop immediately and I thought for a minute that the traffic stop was about to turn into a pursuit when he finally pulled over to the side of the road. The windows on the truck were blacked out and I couldn't see how many people were inside the vehicle.

I got the driver out of the truck because he was acting a little pissy. When he was getting out of the truck, I saw that there were 5 other men inside. I told them to stay inside the vehicle and walked to the side of the road with the driver. He was instantly pissed off because I had stopped him and we were discussing his attitude when he turned to the truck and said something in Spanish.

Suddenly, all of the doors come open on the truck and all 5 of the other men got out despite me telling them not to. The only backup that I had on this particular day was an ancient old "Buford T. Justice" character, who I later found out, was working an off-duty job at the local bank, while on duty, and didn't have his radio on while I was calling for assistance.

I backed up to put distance between the 6 men and myself and drew down on them. I calmly and politely explained to them that I would blow a fucking hole in every one of them that you could drive a cattle truck through, however, they were now spreading out trying to surround me. I was going over in my mind the order in which I would need to shoot these bastards to give me the best chance of survival, when I heard a vehicle come to a sliding stop in the gravel behind me. Needless to say my pucker factor was at about a 9.9 at this point and I was getting a little antsy.

I didn't dare turn around to see who was now behind me, hoping that it was friend and not foe, and suddenly I see them all stop. Their eyes were all looking past me to whoever was behind me. They had stopped advancing on me so I knew I had some help behind me, but I still wasn't going to take my eyes off of them for an instant. Suddenly I hear the unmistakable sound of a shotgun racking and a familiar, gruff voice say *"you need a little help Black?"* It was my friend, the city's Animal Control Officer! My ass was saved by Big Jim that day.

Needless to say, all six of those assholes went to jail for P.O.P (that's "Pissing off the Police" for all you civilians out there). When I finally got back to the station several hours later, ole' Buford T and I had us a little talk to clear the air and I informed him that if he ever left me hanging out to dry again I would kill him myself!

The Animal Control Officer, "Big Jim", backed me up many times during my career working the streets when I had no other help and I am truly grateful to him. His career was cut short when a man hit him as he was walking across the street on the courthouse square. Big Jim's knee was shattered to pieces and he was left permanently handicapped. He served the City of Kaufman for many years and still lives in the area.

Something is not right man...

It was a very dark and foggy night in 1998..... It sounds like the beginning of an Alfred Hitchcock movie, but it is the absolute truth. I was the "OIC" or *Officer in Charge* because the Sergeant had taken the night off and I had more seniority than the other rookie who was working with me. It had been as dead as it could be all night, nothing was moving in town and a dense fog had rolled in. Sometime around midnight we received a report of a prowler at a house on South Dallas Street.

Both of us head over there, mainly because we were both bored to death, and when we get to the area, I made contact with the elderly woman who lived there alone. The small framed woman was visibly shaking while she explained to me that she had heard someone "jiggling" the door handle of her back door. The door was actually on the side of the house and was located under a carport. She said she heard a noise near the door and when she looked, she saw the handle moving around. She told me that she yelled out that she was calling the police and the door handle stopped moving. She then dialed 911.

As we were searching the neighborhood, we received another call about a prowler, this time over on South Houston Street. I sent the other officer to check out that situation while I continued to look around for the suspect on the first call. It was very difficult to see anything because not only was it dark, but the fog was rendering our spotlights useless.

A short time later I heard my partner run a name over the radio. We always ran the complainants so we would have their name for the report. The woman's last name was Murrey. I called my partner to verify who he was dealing with and his confirmation had me instantly shitting bricks. I told him to meet me right away. We met up near the location of the first call and I told him, "*Something is not right man*". He laughed at me and said "what, it's probably kids playing around". I told him, "*Man, my complainant's name on the first call was Murrey. She is William Murrey's mother. The woman you met with is William Murrey's Wife!*"

William Alfred Murrey was locked up in the Kaufman County Jail, which was located in the City of Kaufman, for the rape and murder of 93 year old Rena Ratliff, who had lived two streets over from where we were parked talking. I looked at my partner and said *"you don't think that son of a bitch got out somehow do you?"* Exactly two seconds later my dispatcher called over the radio in a panicked voice *"9117, 9114 come to the station...NOW!"* That's when I knew, we had an escaped murderer creeping around our small town and he was trying to get to his family, whom he had sworn to kill during his trial.

I went to the police department as fast as I could and when I walk in I looked at the Dispatcher Robin Smith and I said *"William Murrey has escaped hasn't he!"* She said "Yes, they don't know how long he has been gone". I told Robin *"He is in town, call everybody that's available and get them in here!"*

I then directed my partner to head back to the house on Houston Street and stay with Murrey's wife. I hauled ass back to his mother's house. I called my Lieutenant, who was the man that worked the murder case against Murrey. His wife answered the phone groggily *"Mrs. Lieutenant, may I speak with LT please it's very important"*. I could hear her trying to wake him up and when he was finally conscious enough to speak he grabbed the phone. "Hello?" *"Lieutenant, William Murrey has escaped from the jail and he is in town somewhere"*……….."WHAT!!!!" Click.

In a matter of about 20 minutes we had every Officer that was on duty either in town or headed to assist us. We tried our best to set up a perimeter around the area between the two houses where we knew he had been. The Sheriff had sent two deputies to watch over Murrey's mother and his wife.

Two blocks east of Murrey's mother's house was the Rand Road trailer park, and directly across the street was a large open field. In the field was an old, half-way demolished wooden building. The area was huge and there were no lights around that location at all. I knew he had to be close because we had been all over the immediate vicinity trying to keep him pinned down.

I started searching the field on foot, flashlight in one hand, gun in the other. I had been walking around, trying to use a grid search technique, in the field for about 15 or 20 minutes and had made my way out close to the middle of the pasture when my flashlight battery went dead (damn unreliable bunny!). After several carefully chosen curse words, I headed back to my car and drove to the station for a fresh battery.

As I was heading back to the field to continue my search, an officer got on the radio "*I think I just saw someone walk across Old Rail Road and into that pasture to the east*". Old Rail Road runs between the field I was searching and a huge hay pasture. I began directing people to different locations in an effort to set up a perimeter around the hay pasture and, hopefully, force him to "lay down" which is cop speak for sit still and try to hide. I ended up positioned exactly halfway down Old Rail Road, between Rand Road and East Mulberry Street. I and a deputy had positioned ourselves where there was a tree line that stretched out into the hay field for about 300 yards. It was eerily dark, foggy, and quiet.

The deputy and I had been in our position for about half an hour, hardly saying a word, while we waited for a team of Bloodhounds from the Coffield Prison Unit to arrive, when suddenly the deputy jumped like somebody had stuck a needle in his left butt-cheek. "*Black!*".... I turned around as fast as I could and saw him pointing toward the tree line. *I saw something move!* He took off in a sprint with me right on his heels. He was running to what looked like a small pile of trash. We were within ten feet of the dark pile when I saw it also. The pile started moving!

Before he could get up to run, the deputy jumped on top of him and I placed the barrel of my Sig Sauer P220 against the gutless coward's forehead and dared him to even fart. We cuffed him up just as it started raining police. When we got him back to the road to put him in a squad car, the Sheriff came over the radio...."*Bring him to my office!*"

The sheriff of Kaufman County back then was known as a man that prisoners didn't want to piss off. (Later on, I heard a rumor that when Murray finally made it back to his new segregated jail cell he looked like he had fallen down a few times). Investigators figured out pretty quickly that he had climbed up into the roof from inside a janitor's closet and crawled out to the lobby area where he had dropped down into the lobby and walked out the front door.

During the debriefing of his escape with Investigators, Murray told the story about how one officer had nearly been right on top of him as he was hiding in a field, "I picked up a broken piece of 2x4 and was getting ready to knock the cop's fucking head off with, but his flashlight went dead". The murderer continued, "He turned around and left and that's the only thing that saved his ass because I wanted his gun". God works in mysterious ways.

On September 17, 2008 at 6:20 p.m. William Alfred Murrey was executed by lethal injection in Huntsville, Texas for the rape and murder of Miss Rena Ratcliff, 93 years of age. I was in Huntsville for his execution.

I need you in route to an animal related call

It was early one Sunday morning and I received an "Animal Related" call on Phillips Circle. I eased that way figuring that this call was exactly like 99% of the other animal related calls; the neighbor's dog was barking or chasing someone's cat.

Now a little information that one needs to know about this story is that the weather on the two days prior to this Sunday was hot, Texas hot! And, as the weather in Texas is prone to do, it had turned cold on this morning.

I turned onto Phillips Circle and there is a woman standing in the street, dressed only in a bathrobe. I pulled up and got out of the patrol car and before I can say anything she says "it's in there!" as she points to the open front door of her house. I ask her what kind of dog it is (because I am assuming it's a dog, remember, it's an "animal related" call). She looks at me like I had just called her kid ugly and says *"Dog!?!? Who said anything about a damned dog....there is a big ass snake in my kitchen!"*

For those of you who don't know me, I'm going to let you in on a little secret.....I am terrified of snakes. I don't just mean regular terrified either, I'm talking "run off and leave your momma" terrified! I don't even like dead snakes. So I did what any grown, self-aware man would do, I turned around without saying a word and walked back to my patrol car. I got in, shut the door, and started the engine. The lady is looking at me like I have lost my mind. Right about then, my Sergeant pulls up (he never learns). He walks up to my car window and asks what is going on. I look him straight in the eyes and say *"she wants to speak to my supervisor"* and I drove away. (I told you I used that tactical maneuver again!)

Come to find out, a neighbor that lived two houses down owned a pet snake. A really large, 8 foot long pet snake. Well, Mr. Giant-Ass Snake had discovered that the roof on his custom built enclosure was left partially open and decided to go check out the cute female down the street. Somehow he managed to get into her kitchen cabinet under the sink and decided to hang out awhile. Apparently, she had intended to clean the tub before taking her morning shower and went to get the cleaning spray from under the kitchen sink.

As she opened the kitchen cabinet, she saw something that didn't look quite right so she bent down to look inside and was staring the reptile right in the face! **She gave the snake the house!**

The owner of the creature went down and reclaimed his "pet" that was large enough to eat a baby hippo, and was promptly cited for "Animal At-Large". I told the guy that he could beat that ticket because his snake was NOT an "animal".....it's a damn dinosaur!

How pissed off can you get at 3 in the morning?

One of the things that we used to like to do when I was working deep nights, was to go out and sit on the "turn around" bridge on Highway 175 and take our breaks, or to meet up to discuss something. One night there were three of us on duty and it had been a very quiet shift up until about 3 a.m. At about that time, I was dispatched to a residence on the north side of town for a 911 hang up. I headed that direction and as I pulled up I noticed that the front door of the residence was standing open (not quite normal for this time of day).

I approached the front of the house and immediately noticed a small child, about 2 or 3 years old sitting on the couch. The child was chewing on a crack pipe. I was looking through the screen door and noticed 2 other small kids playing on the floor in the front room. There were no adults that I could see and there was loud rock & roll music blaring from a radio, somewhere in the back of the house. I called for backup and entered the residence. The first thing I did was take the glass crack pipe away from the little one on the couch, and sit her on the floor, while also trying to keep an eye on the hallway in case someone came around the corner with a damn gun.

I made my way to the edge of the hallway and looked around into the kitchen, which had a full size bed in it! On the bed were two women who were passed out. A quick look around revealed the source of the tunes, a "boom box" radio which was sitting on the back steps and being used to prop open the door to the backyard. There were beer cans everywhere.

I turned and looked down the other end of the hallway and saw three doors. I made my way to the first door which was a bathroom. I then went to the second door which opened into a bedroom. Inside the bedroom was a queen size bed about 4 feet high with an infant lying on the edge of the bed asleep. The baby was about 5 months old.

I moved the baby to the center of the bed and turned her over onto her back, while still trying to watch mine. I then went across the hall to the third door and another bedroom. Inside this room was a 5 year old girl with nothing on but her panties. She was visibly shivering. I went over to cover her up and when I touched her she was on fire! This baby was burning up with fever. It was later discovered that she had been involved in a bad car wreck a couple of weeks before and was having serious complications from her injuries.

All of this had taken place in a matter of seconds, so my backup was still not on scene. I covered up the sick baby and assured her that I would be right back to help her and made my way back down the hallway. My intention at this point was to wake up the two women and slap handcuffs on their asses, however, when I was approaching the bed, I noticed something that caught my eye.

Across the kitchen, on the other side of the room, was a very small hallway containing a washer and dryer. On top of the washer was a can of ice cold beer that still had a small piece of ice sliding down the side of the can, like it had just been taken out of a cooler. I moved closer and saw a door on the other side of the dryer, at the end of the short hallway that I suspected led into the garage. On one side of the narrow area were the washer and dryer and on the other side was an area where clothes were hanging. There was some junk piled up and a couple of laundry baskets sitting on the floor also.

I made my way slowly to the doorway, gun in one hand, flashlight in the other, and slowly began to scan the dark garage from the left to the right. As the beam of my flashlight came around to the right side of the doorway I suddenly noticed someone was standing against the wall inside the garage with something shiny in their hands! I jumped backwards, yelling "SHOW ME YOU FUCKING HANDS!!" But as I stepped back to try and get some distance between us, I tripped over something and went down butt first into one of the laundry baskets! Just then a man, drunk off his ass, stepped out of the dark with a can of beer in his hands. That man will never know how close he came to dying that night.

I managed to crawl out of the laundry basket and "assist" the man to the ground (meaning I slammed his ass so hard on the floor that his grandchildren felt it!). I then handcuffed him and drug him by his feet all the way out to the front yard. He was cussing and threatening me the entire way. My backup officers were arriving about that time and when they saw me dragging this idiot out of the house and down the front porch stairs by his feet, they knew something was up, you know, "police intuition" and all.

I yelled at the first officer to go inside and wake up the two passed out skanks in the kitchen and take them into custody. I then told the second officer to call for an ambulance and go take care of the sick little girl in the back bedroom. I went out and checked the backyard but found nothing but a million empty beer cans and liquor bottles thrown all over the yard. The words to describe how angry I was at this point have not been invented yet!

To this day, I know there was another man inside that house when I got there. He must have run out to the backyard when he heard me come in. That ice cold beer can sitting on the washer possibly saved me from a very uncomfortable situation.

All in all there were 6 kids in the house, all under the age of 6. I kept tabs on those kids for a long time after that. They were all eventually placed into the care of maternal or paternal grandparents, and the adults that were found inside the house were all sentenced to short prison stays for child endangerment. The sick little girl received the medical attention that she desperately needed and recovered very well. We never did identify the other individual.

As a side note, I was awarded a commendation for my actions and the report that I wrote on this case. I very much appreciated the department recognizing me, but what I have kept with me from this incident was the fact that I sincerely believe I made a difference in those children's lives that night. Nothing else compares to that.

Where are your clothes man?!?

Oooooh yeeaahh..... Someone's doing something they shouldn't be doing! Those were my thoughts as I was driving into City Lake Park one Sunday afternoon and saw two trucks parked at the back of the park, near the boat ramp area. The trucks were parked about 30 feet apart from one another, which was odd, but they were definitely together.

I made my way back to where the trucks were parked and ran both license plates before getting out and making my approach. I was not trying to be sneaky or quiet; I was moving and walking just like I did during any other regular traffic contact. I approached the driver's side of the closest truck and when I looked inside..............good googilly goo!!!!!

She was lying on her back with her head against the driver's door with one foot on the dash and the other on the top of the seat. He was crouched down between her legs and going at it like a bulldog eating a pot pie! If he had opened his eyes he would be staring me in the face. It was readily apparent that she was thoroughly enjoying his talents and didn't have a care in the world, other than to get where she was going.

They were both completely naked and when I say naked, I mean "Nekkid". She didn't even have toenail polish on! I tapped on the window, which was actually rolled down about 2 inches from the top...nothing. I tapped again.......nothing. I cleared my throat loudly.......nothing. So finally I just said "*HEY!*"

She opened her eyes and looked straight up into my smiling face. He had not heard me and continued working on his project, so she reached down and smacked him on his head. He opened his eyes, saw my smiling face, and jumped up like a St. Bernard had just cold-nosed him square in the sack!

At this point, she was desperately trying to get her clothes on while he was just sitting there looking incredibly disappointed. I told him to get dressed and he looked down and mumbled "I can't officer, I don't have my clothes". Thinking this was quite strange, I said "Where are your clothes man?" He replied sheepishly "they are over there in my truck" pointing at the second truck about 30 feet away.

Now, about this time, there are several questions going through my head, but the first one I want an answer to is "*Are you telling me that you got butt-naked in your truck and walked across all of those rocks to get into her truck?*" To which he states "Yes sir". Question #2 "*WHY?*" He starts explaining "well I was already here waiting on her and I was kinda horny so I went ahead and got my clothes off so that when she got here I wouldn't have to waste any time. But then she pulled up way over here, so instead of waiting on her to pull over closer, I just got out and came over here to her"....... *Well just damn!*

The boat ramp area of Kaufman's City Lakes Park where I seemed to always find people playing "Hide-the-Pickle". Photo by Edward Black.

Rather than continue this line of questioning with him sitting there in his birthday suit, I told him "Get *to steppin! I'm not going to get em for you*". So he got out of the truck and slowly, painfully began the walk of shame across a rock parking lot to get his clothes so we could continue our meeting of the minds.

I then tell the woman, who has since managed to put on her panties and tank-top, to get out of the truck. As she opens the door I see an open bottle of whiskey in the floorboard and a rather large, bright purple dildo on the seat. I asked her if there was anything, other than the whiskey, in the truck that I needed to know about, to which she replied "well uh, there is nothing illegal, but there are some embarrassing items in there". "*Uh, huh…….okay then*". So being the dutiful, good little cop that I am, and in the interest of a complete and thorough investigation, I absolutely had to know what these items were.

It would take another chapter of this book to describe each individual item that I found, so let's just suffice it to say that this young lady had decided to bring along her entire, generous collection of sex toys for this rendezvous! After making sure there were no drugs or weapons inside the vehicle, I told her to get back in and finish getting dressed and refocused my attention on Shoeless Joe Jackson.

After performing the same search on his truck and only finding his collection of "Toes are Tasty" fetish magazines, I issued them a few citations and sent them on their way. Little did I know that this was the beginning of a very eventful summer for me when it came to catching people playing hide the pickle in public!

Death in the Garden Center

On Tuesday, March 22 of 2016 John Morgan went to work like he did any other day. He clocked in, and reported to his assigned work area in the Garden Center of the Walmart in Kaufman. Less than 2 hours later a gunman walked in through the Garden Center doors, walked past a display of Round Up weed killer and circled around behind Morgan. *"Hey, is your name John?"* he asked just before he stuck a Taurus PT 24/7 Pro to the back of Morgan's head, and ended his life with the squeeze of one finger.

The gunman, Donald Ray Coleman, then stuck the gun to his head and pulled the trigger once more in an attempt to take the coward's way out. It didn't work. Coleman was such a loser that he couldn't even kill himself correctly.

When I arrived on scene less than 2 minutes after the shooting, I could still smell the gunpowder in the air. Both of the men were lying on the floor, bleeding profusely from head wounds. There were several employees that were screaming and crying. I pointed at a store supervisor and ordered him to take the women outside and stay with them. I pointed at two officers and told them each to stand by the entrance doors that led into the Garden Center and not let anyone in unless they absolutely had to be in there. I grabbed an officer from another agency that had arrived and told him to tape off the entire area with crime scene tape.

As the ambulance crew was coming in the doors I directed one of my Investigators to go to the Asset Protection office to view and obtain video of the offense. This I knew would be the single most important piece of evidence that we would be able to get our hands on so I wanted it sooner, rather than later.

The store had been evacuated as soon as the shots were fired, an impressive feat under any circumstance, but especially under these conditions. With everyone outside, I became concerned about key witnesses leaving before we could speak to them. I grabbed another officer from a neighboring agency and instructed him to go out and gather all of the witnesses together in one place.

A couple of minutes later, as I was standing there waiting for the paramedics to finish working on the assassin, when a team of DPS Tactical Officers came barreling through the door with assault rifles. I threw my arms up to stop them and told them that the shooter was down, there were no more suspects in the store, and that they needed to back out of my crime scene. They all looked at me like I had just kicked their new puppy.

While I was inside the store dealing with the crime scene, the Kaufman County Sheriff Department's Public Information Officer (PIO) released a statement to the media that the shooter was deceased. I found out about this when an alert popped up on my cell phone from NBC ...."**Gunman opens fire at Walmart in Kaufman. Employee and shooter dead**".

This came as quite a surprise to me for several reasons, not the least of which was that I was standing there watching EMT's working on him because he *WAS* alive. Also because, KSO had nothing to do with the investigation at that time. It was my case, in my city, and I was the PIO for the Kaufman Police Department and the only one, other than the Chief of Police, who is authorized to speak to reporters. Why the hell the Sheriff's Department would even speak to the press regarding this incident was beyond me and it royally pissed me off.

When I was finally able to go out and address the crowd of reporters to tell them what information we could release, I was asked several times where the confusion came regarding the shooter being alive or dead. What the hell do you say to that to try and keep the peace between your agency and a neighboring agency that clearly crossed established lines and fucked up?

I decided to be diplomatic about it, so I just explained to them that sometimes in the confusion of an active situation like this; the wrong information can get passed around. Luckily, after they realized that they weren't going to get anything else out of me, they accepted my excuse.

The investigation later revealed that Mr. Morgan had been dating Coleman's ex-wife and he couldn't stand it. Just weeks before this heinous act, Coleman was suspected of shooting up Morgan's truck as it sat in the driveway of his Gun Barrel City home. He had also recently been accused of stealing Morgan's boat from him and dumping it on a dirt road.

An aerial view of the shooting scene. You can see my vehicle (White Crown Vic) in the center of the photo.
Photo Credit, MyFoxDFW.com

Coleman not only terrorized John Morgan, he also harassed and stalked his ex-wife. Their relationship was a volatile one. After she had left him, he broke into her house, kidnapped her, and drug her out to a barn on the property. There, he tied her up with plans to do who-knows-what, but she managed to escape before he could follow through with his intentions. He was a real asshole.

Morgan was pronounced deceased at the scene. Coleman had survived his lame attempt at suicide and was transported to a Dallas hospital, where he eventually recovered with minimal lasting effects from the bullet to his head. He was certainly healthy enough to go to prison anyway.

On May 18, 2017 Donald Ray Coleman pled guilty to the murder of John Morgan and was sentenced to 38 years in prison. He must serve half his sentence before he becomes eligible for parole. He is currently serving his time at the Neal Unit in Amarillo, Texas.

Finally Justice-
A 22 Year Old Cold Case Solved

On a warm Thursday night in June of 1994, there was not a lot going on in Kaufman, Texas. Most of the kids liked to hang out at the City Coin Laundry building at the corner of South Washington and West Fourth Street. One of those sitting around talking was Francisco Sanchez Salazar, another was Alvaro Iglesias. The two did not like each other and frequently got into fights.

No one knows for sure how the two ended up in the alley behind the laundromat and the building next door, but suddenly the sound of what seemed like non-stop gunshots filled the night. People fell to the ground; some ran behind cars to take cover. Two men in a pickup driving by stated that they saw Alvaro Iglesias running from the scene with a gun in his hand. When the officers arrived they found Francisco Salazar with 14 bullet holes in his body.

Kaufman Police Detective Thomas Bohn investigated the case and was able to obtain a warrant for the arrest of Iglesias; however, 2 days after the murder Alvaro Iglesias quietly slipped across the border into Mexico and was not seen again.......that is until twenty-two years later on September 28, 2016.

In August of 2016 Kaufman County Law Enforcement, along with Kaufman County Crime Stoppers, started publishing a "Top 10 Most Wanted" list. When they called me and asked our agency to participate, I knew exactly who I wanted to put out there.

I was always a student of Criminal Investigations. I would spend a lot of time reading old cases that had been worked in the past trying to get to know the techniques and tactics used to solve crimes by the Investigators that had come before me. Many times during my career, I would go in and pull the file of Kaufman's only unsolved murder case and look it over. I always hoped that something would jump out at me that would help us make an arrest, but it never did. I went to the file room and once again retrieved that old, worn manila folder. I thumbed through the two inches of documents and pulled out the small black and white photo of Alvaro Iglesias as a 23 year old kid. I then submitted it to the Kaufman County Crime Stoppers board for publishing on the newly created Most Wanted list.

A few weeks went by with no bites but then one morning I opened my email and couldn't believe it, Crime Stoppers had received a tip about our case. I opened the tip and read the contents........Iglesias was living in Wichita, Kansas under the name Mauricio San Miguel Reyes. That's pretty much all it said. Knowing that the information in the tip was a long shot, I walked over to the Criminal Investigations office and explained to Sergeant Tommy Black (no relation) about the tip. "*See what you can find out*".

The only photo of the suspect, Alvaro Iglesias Rodriguez that the Kaufman Police Department had from the original case file.

A couple of days later, I received another email. This time it described the vehicle that Iglesias was supposed to be driving. A few days after that, a third tip, this time with an address. Now things were getting interesting!

The problem we faced was that we had absolutely no way to prove that Reyes was actually Alvaro Iglesias. The Kaufman Police Department had never arrested Alvaro Iglesias before the murder, so we didn't have his fingerprints on file. What the hell were we going to do now?!?

I called in Sgt. Black and told him I wanted him to go over to the sheriff's department where his cousin, Robert, happened to be in charge of the department's Property and Evidence Division. I wanted them to go through the sheriff department's old arrest files and see if by any luck, they might have arrested Alvaro Iglesias sometime before the murder took place and before he fled to Mexico. I knew finding such a file, if it even existed, would be a million-to-one shot, but we didn't have a lot of other options at that point.

Tommy Black and KSO Sgt. Robert McGee physically searched through an old storage container that was parked out behind the jail and went through dozens of boxes containing thousands of old files and suddenly they hit the jackpot! They discovered a single arrest file for Iglesias and inside was an old, yellowing fingerprint card! The fingerprints on the 8X8 piece of cardboard were still remarkably good condition. Those loops, hooks, and whirls were the missing piece of the puzzle.

The telephone lines between Kaufman, Texas and Wichita, Kansas were on fire for the next few days. Wichita Police had arrested Iglesias (under the name "Mauricio San Miguel Reyes") more than once which meant they had his fingerprints. A day later, we had the results of the fingerprint comparison......*THEY MATCHED!*
After a brief celebration, I turned and looked at my two young Detectives, Tommy Black and Jason Stastny, and asked them *"What are ya'll doing standing here all happy?!? Get your asses to Kansas and go get our murderer!"*

Officers were spread out all over the neighborhood in unmarked cars. They were told that the suspect would be home at 5 o'clock. At almost exactly 5 p.m. a truck pulled over at the corner down the street and the target got out. He started walking toward his residence but didn't get far. Officers with the Wichita, Kansas Police Department S.W.A.T. Team swarmed in and had handcuffs on him before he knew what hit him. The two Kaufman Detectives could barely contain their excitement!

Iglesias was arrested and taken to the Wichita Police Department. He believed at the time that he had only been arrested on a misdemeanor warrant for assault. They placed him in an interview room where Sergeant Stastny went in to speak with him. When Stastny informed him that he was an Investigator from Kaufman, Texas he stared for a brief moment and then dropped his head and refused to speak. The ghost of Francisco Sanchez Salazar that had been chasing him for 22 years had just caught up to him and he knew it.

When he refused to speak with the Investigators, they did the next best thing; they went to see his family. Once they arrived at the modest framed home, Sergeants Black and Stastny introduced themselves to the family and told them where they were from. At that moment, the air was sucked out of the room. His mother started crying. Tears welled up in his father's tired, experienced eyes. The Detectives stood there quietly, trying to figure out why his parents had instantly reacted the way they did..."*Could they possibly know about the murder?*"

Incredibly, Iglesias' mother looked at her husband and stated "*You tell them papa, you know the story best*". The Detectives couldn't believe what they were hearing! After speaking with the family of the man they had just arrested for murder it became apparent. The entire family knew that their son, brother, husband, and father had killed a man in Texas in 1994 and had kept that secret for all those years.

Iglesias' father told his painful story to the two officers. He stated that on the night of the murder his son had come running into the house screaming that he had shot Francisco and he needed to get out of Kaufman fast. The family then packed him some clothes and drove south through the night. Two days later, they helped him stealthily get across the Rio Grande River. Three years later, Iglesias illegally crossed back into the United States and made his way to Kansas where he and his family had been living in the City of Wichita ever since, constantly looking over their shoulders.

I cannot accurately describe the sense of pride and satisfaction that I feel when I think about this "Cold Case" and its resolution. Tommy Black and Jason Stastny worked their asses off on this case, along with Kandice Machala, my CID Secretary. Without the assistance of the fine men and women at the Wichita Police Department, a murderer would still be out living the good life. Robert McGee at the Kaufman County Sheriff Department was a huge help as well. Officer Thomas Bohn, the original Investigator on this case back in 1994, had left the department for several years and then returned and was working with us during the time this case was resolved. He was a tremendous asset in bringing this suspect to justice.

Alvaro Iglesias Rodriguez was extradited back to Texas and soon after entered into a plea agreement with the District Attorney's office. He agreed to plead guilty to Murder in exchange for a 10 year prison sentence. Many people were angry about the light sentence but they shouldn't have been. When you think about it from a prosecution standpoint, we had no evidence, no witnesses, and no forensics. It would have been hard as hell to obtain a conviction if this case had gone to trial. At least with the plea deal, he had to see the inside of a Texas prison cell with plenty of time to think about nothing but what had put him in there.

The only part of this entire case that bothers me is the fact that we have been unable to track down and make contact with any of Francisco Sanchez Salazar's family. We have been unable to give them the news and, just maybe, some closure. I hope when his mother and father, and the rest of his family, are reunited with him one day, that they appreciate how hard we worked to bring justice to their family.

I'm sure they will.

*Booking photo of Alvaro Iglesias Rodriguez.
Photo credit, Wichita, Kansas Police Department.*

He may be small, but he's got Meth on his side!

I was working an off-duty security job at the Kaufman Brookshires grocery store one evening when one of the clerks told me that he had witnessed a man place two boxes of Benadryl into his shirt and he was heading for the doors on the other end of the building. Meth dealers, and users, are always stealing Benadryl, and any other medicines, that contain pseudoephedrine, a key ingredient in Methamphetamine.

I quickly went outside and spotted the person the clerk was talking about. He was a short, thin man who probably didn't weigh 120 pounds soaking wet. I caught up to him just as he was about to get into his car and explained to him that he needed to come with me back inside the store. I could easily see the shapes of the boxes of Benadryl through his shirt.

Reluctantly, he agreed and walked all the way back into the store and into the security office with me. I shut the door and told him to have a seat in one of the plastic chairs next to the desk. It was a small office containing a desk with a computer, a couple of chairs, and a tall metal stand that held numerous VCR's, video monitors, and other video recording devices.

I asked him what his name was and told him to go ahead and open his shirt and give me the stuff that he had stolen. He denied stealing anything even after I told the brain surgeon that I could read the boxes through his shirt. Eventually he decided that this strategy wasn't working for him and he gave me the Benadryl.

He was still sitting there as calm as a drunk hobo, apologizing for his momentary lapse in judgement, when I told him that he was under arrest and I needed him to stand up, turn around, and place his hands behind his back. As I reached to grab him, all hell broke loose!

He bolted for the door and hit me across the nose with his fist. I latched on to him around the waist trying to get him down on the floor. He bounced me off of every wall in that office! We knocked the computer off the desk, pictures off the walls, a monitor fell off of the metal computer rack when we slammed into it and went into pieces when it hit the floor.

He was still trying to escape as I yelled at him *"your ass is not getting out of this office!"* The next thing I know, we are outside the office rolling around on the floor with a dozen employees and customers watching in disbelief.

I was getting tired but he was hopped up on Meth and was not about to give up. I was down on the floor with him punching and kicking me and me trying to get him in a headlock. Suddenly I was staring him in the crotch. He had made it to his feet and I had only one shot. I lunged up between his legs with my right arm and nailed him with a solid fist to the crown jewels!

He went down long enough for me to catch a breath or two and then, to my disbelief, he was fighting to get up again. I had smashed his nuts flat and he was still able to fight! I was just about spent when I see the Assistant Manager, John, come flying around the corner like a bull. He was a very large man, about 6'3 and 240 pounds. He just barreled into both of us, sprawling all of us out onto the tiled floor like bowling pins.

At this point, I was finally able to get the little bastard in a headlock, so as I was doing my best to choke his ass out cold, I reached back on my duty belt, grabbed my handcuffs and threw them at the big man, *"put those on this strong son-of-a-bitch and fast!"*

As soon as I heard that second cuff click I just fell back in complete exhaustion. After a few minutes, I got up and looked myself over. My shirt was torn, my badge was hanging half-way off my uniform, my pants were ripped at the knee, and my nose was bleeding. Meth-man didn't look much better.

A short time later one of our officers came in the door and took custody of the suspect. As we were walking him out to the car for his trip to jail, he jerked away from the other officer and took off running with his hands cuffed up behind his back! He made it about 20 feet before he was caught from behind and fell face-first onto the blacktop parking lot.

After an ambulance had arrived and checked him over real good, he was finally taken to the Kaufman County Law Enforcement Center and booked in. The jailers had to strap the dumbass in a restraint chair because he was still determined not to go into the jail cell.

This was not the only time that I had my ass whipped, but it was one of the worst. I'm not angry about that, but I'm still pissed that he got out of that office! He made a liar out of me.

The Bloody Van...

I was working traffic on Highway 175 one rainy and cold night. I clocked an old White colored GMC Van traveling westbound at about 13 miles over the speed limit. It was the kind of old van that doesn't have any windows on the sides, but has two doors with windows on the back of it.

As I caught up with the van I noticed that there was some kind of dark colored liquid pouring out from under the doors on the back of the van. As I got closer, the liquid was splashing all over the hood and windshield of my squad. I could see through the rear windows what looked like several people in the back of the van moving around.

I lit the vehicle up for a traffic stop and the van pulled over under what we called the "turn-around bridge". I notified dispatch of my location and got out of my car. As I started approaching the van, I realized that the dark colored liquid that I was seeing was actually dark red, but it wasn't paint............*oh shit, it's blood!!*

"Dispatch send me some more units code 3!!" I backed up to my patrol car and drew my weapon. The driver of the van started to get out but I stated politely *"get your ass back in that van and don't you move until I tell you too!"* I guess he detected something in the tone of my voice that made him feel like he needed to do as I asked because he did just that without question.

My sergeant and another officer soon arrived to assist me. I informed them that I have no idea what is going on but the van is bleeding! They looked at me kind of funny but then realized that I wasn't shitting them. We approached the van and got the driver out first; we then removed the front passenger and could hear several more people moving around inside the van. As I opened the sliding side door of the van there were four other men in the van and they were all covered in blood...........pig blood.

These six brain surgeons had been wild hog hunting and had butchered several large hogs. They then put all of the meat inside these huge pots that they filled with the hogs' blood, but they didn't have any lids on the pots. The hog blood had splashed all over the van, all over them, and they were all having a blast because all of them, except the driver, were drunk off their asses and laughing like teenage school girls!

After checking everything out, and getting past being the butt of all the other officer's jokes, I spoke with the driver and politely told him to get him and his blood-soaked, drunk-ass, giggling, hog-hunting friends out of my city and to do it fast!

Cops can come across almost anything when they stop a vehicle, but I'm pretty sure there are not many that have ever stopped a bleeding van!

Having a Gay Old Time!

I had just left the Kaufman County Jail and was headed back to the Police Department. I was sitting at the crossover on Highway 175 waiting for traffic to clear when I noticed a 4-door pickup run off onto the shoulder of the road. The driver quickly jerked the truck back into his lane of traffic but almost hit the car beside him. I had to check this out and make sure the driver wasn't intoxicated so I caught up to the vehicle and pulled them over near the Houston Street exit.

As I was walking up to the driver's door I could hear the people in the truck laughing like crazy. I noticed the driver was rolling down all of the windows so when I reached the rear door I looked in the backseat and instantly asked myself why in the hell I ever become a cop!

Sitting in the middle of the backseat was a completely naked man, bound and tied up with rope. I eased my right hand down and removed my weapon from its holster, but everyone in the truck, including the tied up naked dude, were laughing their asses off.

I slowly made my way up to the driver's door and advised the man sitting there that he should probably start explaining to me what the hell was going on, and while he did so, he might want to keep his hands where I could see them. I was relieved to see that the two guys in the front were at least dressed.

He started explaining to me that a large group of friends from a gay club in Dallas had held a weekend-long party at a house on Cedar Creek Lake to celebrate their "hostage's" recent promotion at work. Apparently, the party was now shifting back to the club in Dallas, and their friend in the backseat had told them that he needed to go home and get some rest. Well, being the good friends that they were, they decided to strip him of his clothes so he couldn't leave, and then tied him up to transport him back to party headquarters.

Uh-Huh..........

I identified everybody and asked Mr. Hostage if he was being held against his will or if he was going along with the kidnapping, to which he assured me that I did not need to rescue him and then thanked me for giving them a story to tell for the rest of their lives.

This job is interesting I will say that!

Pumping Away at the Pump House!

About two miles outside of Kaufman to the east there is an old lake. The entrance to the lake off of Highway 243 is a dirt road that winds back down through some trees before coming to a dead end at the water. There is an old pump station out there where kids have swam, drank beer, smoked dope, and had sex for many years. It is an old tan colored brick structure with graffiti spray painted all over it. The actual pump house sits out about 40 feet on a pier of sorts. The only way to get out to the pump house is to climb up onto the pier from an embankment and then walk out to it.

The City of Kaufman owns this property and we are required to patrol it so I tried to make it out there at least a couple of times per shift. It was not unusual to catch teenagers out there partying and making out, and it was very popular with the dope-heads.

One afternoon, I made my way out to the "243 Lake" for a security check and noticed a car and a pickup both parked in the tall weeds near the pier of the pump house. I drove over a little closer to the water where I could see most of the pier but was unable to see anybody. I checked out with dispatch and started walking over to where the vehicles were parked. As I got closer, I saw that the truck was one of a local plumbing company's trucks. There was nobody inside either vehicle.

I continued making my way over to the pier, going around a clump of trees and walking up onto an embankment, before I was able to spot the two people who belonged to the vehicles. And boy did I spot them!

She was lying on her back on the concrete pier and he was doing his best to knock the bottom completely out of it! She was a bigger girl and he was a small, skinny man and if ever I saw a guy with a case of "little man syndrome" it was him! Hell, he was pounding it so hard he was making waves in the water 15 feet below!

Now, the funny thing is, all of their clothes were in a pile at the front of the pier where I was at. They were all the way down at the pump house about 40 feet away bumping uglies like cavemen!

I started trying to get their attention and then realized that the wind was blowing off of the water toward me, and it was blowing pretty good. It was going to be difficult for them to hear me unless I yelled really loudly or walked down there. I thought about it and decided that it would be less embarrassing for them if I just yelled to get their attention....

Pump house at the 243 Lake
Photo by Edward Black

So as I was walking toward them I was waiting for them to look up and see me, but neither one of them ever did. There were wasps and bees flying all around that pump house, but a giant swarm of Africanized Killer Bees couldn't have stopped him from unclogging that drain he was working on.

I got about 5 feet from them before I finally say "Excuse me!" And they both turn and look at me like they were staring at a ghost. I said "Mind if I interrupt you for a minute?" And Lord bless her, she was trying everything in the book to hide what she had but as soon as she would cover up one part, another part would jump out! So, I told them to go on down and put their clothes on and then we would talk.

After they got dressed and I obtained their ID's both of them at the same time said "Please don't run us over the radio Officer". I asked what the problem was (even though I already knew that they were both married, just not to each other) and he say's "well we are kind of sneaking around and both of our spouses have scanners at home, and we know lots of people in town also". I knew where they both worked and lived (I saw them almost every day when I was working) so I cut them a break and told them to find a better place to do their sneaking around.

I'll give him credit though. He looked like a Dachshund humping a St. Bernard but he never quit on it!

Neither Snow nor Rain nor Heat nor Gloom of Night....

This particular summer that I was working Patrol was unlike anything seen before in the history of police work. Well, not really, but it was crazy how many times I caught people having sex in public places in those few months. My call number was 905 and I caught so many people in the act, that the dispatchers renamed the code for "Public Lewdness" to "905".

Once again, I go back out to the "Old 243 Lake" for a security check and observe a car parked by the water. It immediately becomes apparent exactly what the occupants of the car are doing because the female is in the center of the backseat, facing the opposite direction, and bouncing up and down rather quickly, oh, and she is completely butt-naked.

I honked the horn to let them know that they had an audience; however, they were listening to a tune of their own and did not pay any attention to mine. I walked up to the passenger side of the car and, as expected, there was a very pleased looking young man sitting in the center of the backseat with his legs outstretched between the 2 front seats, over the center console. She was riding him like a PBR Champion riding Bodacious!

What I noticed next was the small video camera that they had set up on top of the front seat that was recording their little rodeo. I tapped on the glass and she turned her head and rolled off of him as fast as she could. He was left sitting there with his little soldier saluting the world.

I let them get dressed and got them out of the car. I made him stand at the rear of the car while I took her over by my vehicle to ask the standard questions....Are you here because you want to be...Are you here voluntarily....and so on.

It was then that I realized that I knew her. She was my local Mail Carrier! I also knew where she, *and her husband*, lived. I then went and spoke with Bodacious and he had the same standard answers as to why they were there and what they were doing. I went back to the embarrassed mail lady and asked her about the video camera. Her reply was "yeah, he likes to record us and then watch it while we talk on the phone".

Well alrighty then.

I advised them to find a more private spot better suited for their filmmaking activities and sent them on their way.

From that day forward my mail was always delivered early for some reason.

The 243 Lake area where there was always something interesting going on.
Photo by Edward Black

I dropped my keys...

All throughout this particular summer I had been trying to catch the men that were using the city's playground restrooms for a place to meet up and have sex with each other. The restroom facilities are located less than 30 feet from the kid's playground so I was determined to put a stop to it. I had been told that this was happening during the day, so I started heavily patrolling the park and monitoring the graffiti that was being written on the restroom walls. These guys were brazen; some of them would put their telephone numbers on the wall, dates and times to meet them at the park, etc.

I investigated numerous telephone numbers that I found written in the bathrooms and several of them came back to addresses within the city, so I had a pretty good idea what type of cars and trucks that I was looking for.

One morning, a couple of days after I had met the mail lady, I was at the station when a call came in regarding a welfare concern at the park. The caller stated that two men had gone into the bathroom together and had been in there a long time. *I WAS OUT THE DOOR AND GONE IN SECONDS!*

I raced to the park and was relieved when I pulled in and got close enough to the parking lot to see that there were still two vehicles parked there. Two of the vehicles that I had been watching! I parked my car and turned my portable radio down all the way. I didn't want to take a chance on tipping them off that I was there. I quietly walked (ok, maybe ran a little) up to the bathroom door and jerked it open as quickly as I could. BUSTED!

One man was standing up against the wall "receiving" and the other was on his knees "giving". I scared them both so badly it's a miracle the giver didn't bite it off! I told them to get their asses out of there and put their hands on the wall. I handcuffed them both and called for two wreckers to impound their cars.
Both of them went to jail, one happy, one not so happy.

A couple of days later I was called to the station by the Chief of Police and asked to meet him in his office. When I walked in I saw Mr. Giver sitting there.

Me: Yes sir Chief?
Chief: Ed, Mr. Giver here says that you were mistaken in what you saw the other day at the bathroom in the park.
Me: Really? How so?
Chief: Yes, he says that he had dropped his keys in the bathroom and was simply bending down picking them up when you opened the door. Is it possible that is what happened?
Me: Well Sir, he certainly could have dropped his keys while in the (single stall) bathroom with another man, and he could have certainly bent down to pick them up. My question would be "how did the other man's penis fall into his mouth while this was happening?"
Chief: You are excused Ed, thank you".

The next day, Mr. Giver's wife came to the station and asked to speak to me. She was a cool lady with a heavy British accent and she had a "no bullshit" way about her. She explained to me that her husband was claiming that he got arrested because he was caught masturbating in the park. She stated that she believed this to be a damned lie and asked me to tell her what happened. Keep in mind, this was before "open records" became such a big issue and we could actually speak with people and tell them the truth about things.

I told her what had happened and she said "I fucking knew it!" She went on to tell me that he had been arrested a few years before at a park in Houston with several men, but claimed that he was just in the wrong place at the wrong time. I explained to her as gently as I could that she needed to be tested for STD's, especially HIV, because he had been doing this for a long time and this was by no means his first rodeo. She also told me that he was a missionary in their church and was scheduled to leave to go to Venezuela the next week; however, she intended full well to "put a stop to the sorry cock-sucking bloke going anywhere with her or the church". I liked this lady!

I never heard from or saw Mr. Giver after that, but I did run into his wife a few years later and she and her kids were doing very well. Mr. Receiver just took his punishment and went on about his business. He didn't give a damn who knew about it. I was told that several years later he was sent to prison on fraud charges.

That was the first and only time I was able to make an arrest at that park of men "hooking up" there, I guess word got out that I was working that location pretty hard (no pun intended), and they decided to go somewhere else for their playtime.

He's a friend of the family

Are they fighting? Are they dancing? Are they wrestling with a large bear? Nope, they are having sex in the front seat of a Toyota Corolla.

I rolled up on this car at the park, in broad daylight, and all I can see is a giant ass going up and down in the windshield of the tiny car! And when I say "going up and down" I mean, "rising above the dashboard" up and down!

She was a rather large girl, 18 years old, and the upstairs matched the downstairs. He, once I could finally see him, was tall, skinny, 53 years old, and hung like a Mississippi mule. Both were from Terrell, just up the road about 12 miles.

Me: Umm, ma'am how old are you?
Her: "I'm 18"
Me: And how old is your friend?
Her: "He is 53"
Me: Uh-huh. Is he your boyfriend?
Her: "No, he's just a friend of the family."
Me: Okay then.

That is how it went for several minutes. She explained to me that he was a friend of her family's and that his wife wouldn't have sex with him anymore, so she took care of his needs and he took care of hers. After many more questions to make sure she was of sound mind, and was not being forced to be there with him, I had no choice but to send them back up the road to Terrell. She said they needed to get back anyway because they were only supposed to be running to the store.

The Sugar-daddy sat there smiling his ass off the entire time.

The Story of Kelley Osgan

When I first became a Kaufman Police Officer, I quickly came to know a young lady named Kelley. Kelley was just a child, but had already lived a hard life, despite her grandfather being a member of our police department. He did what he could do for her, but Kelley was destined to be a statistic from the get-go.

Crack Cocaine was Kelley's drug of choice and it was what ultimately led to her death, in more ways than one. The cheap and readily available drug took a once beautiful and intelligent young lady and turned her into a $10 crack whore. I had issued her so many tickets for possession of drug paraphernalia that you could fill a large mailbox with them all. It finally got to the point where, when I saw her walking down the road, I would simply pull up and say "take out your crack pipe and bust it on the ground Kelley". She always would, without argument and then be on her way. There were times when I would make her destroy 3 or 4 pipes in a single day! I had no idea where she would come up with them all; it was like she had her own crack pipe warehouse!

I tried time and time again to get Kelley into a drug rehab program, but after every stay she would come out and head straight for her dealers. The evil substance wouldn't let go of her and she couldn't let go of it.

Kelley hooked up with a man we will call Lennie. Lennie truly loved Kelley, in the only ways he knew how. Every time you saw Kelley, you would see Lennie walking 20 feet behind her. Most of the time she was cursing at him or yelling at him for whatever imagined wrong she had felt that day. Lennie and she lived under a local drunk's carport for months at a time, Sometimes, if Kelley "treated him well", he would allow them to come in and take a shower, but that did not happen very often.

I would talk to Lennie sometimes and he would tell me how much it hurt him that Kelley was always having sex with other men just to get drugs or a little cash and he would tell me how much he wanted to find a way to get her out of that life and into a better one. I truly did feel sorry for Lennie.

After all of the years of being with Kelley, taking care of her, doing drugs with her, and sleeping under carports with her, it almost seemed unfair that Lennie was serving time in the Kaufman County Jail when she was killed*. On the other hand, it was probably a good thing for him in the long run, because he would have been put through the ringer as a suspect. However, if he had been out on the streets with her, maybe her life wouldn't have ended the way it did.
*I will tell you about the murder of Kelley later in this book.

One afternoon, about a year before she was murdered, I was doing my routine patrols and drove out to the "Old 243 Lake" to see what mischief was taking place. As I was driving down the dirt road and came into view of the main parking area, I saw a truck parked facing me. I then saw a man standing beside the truck, on the passenger side, with the door open and suddenly a young lady rises up and is sitting in the passenger seat.

The man quickly slams the door of his truck, runs around and gets into the driver's seat and begins heading toward me, leaving the lake area (Because, you know, that doesn't look suspicious) As the truck passes me, I realize that it is Kelley sitting in the passenger seat and I have never seen the driver before.......... *OH HELL NO!*

I turned around and started after the truck. By the time I had made it out to the main road, the truck was hauling ass east on Highway 243. It took me a few miles to catch them, but I soon did and made a traffic stop on the truck.

I ordered the driver to exit his vehicle and walk back toward me. He did as directed and, after I patted him down for weapons, we had us a little talk.

Me: Hello, what's your name?
Him: Uh, hey. My name is Mark.
Me: Who is the young lady in the truck Mark?
Him: Oh she's just a friend.
Me: What's her name?
Him: Uh, I think its Kelley.
Me: You "think" it's Kelley? I thought she was your friend?
Him: Uh, aww hell Officer, you know what was going on.
Me: Yeah, but why don't you explain it to me anyway.

Him: We were, uh, you know, having sex.
Me: Why were you at the place where I saw you back there? Why aren't you at your house?
Him: Well, uh, I was just driving down the road and she flagged me down and asked me if I wanted to have some fun.
Me: Have some fun?
Him: Yes sir, so I asked her how much and she said $10. She got in and told me where to drive to. That's how we ended up back there where you saw us.
Me: Did you pay her?
Him: Yes sir.
Me: What did you use to pay her and where did she put it?
Him: I gave her a $10 bill and she put it in her front right pocket.
Me: I'm going to give you this form; I want you to write me out a statement of what you just told me. After that I will decide whether or not I am going to take you to jail, understand?
Him: Yes sir, no problem.

I then went up and politely asked Kelley to get out of the truck. She and I then had a conversation that went like this:

Me: Hello Kelley
Her: Hey Officer Black
Me: Whatcha doin?
Her: Oh just riding around with my friend
Me: Oh yeah, what's your friend's name?
Her: His name is Mark.
Me: Nice try Kelley, His name is not Mark.
Her: Well that's what he told me it was!
Me: How long have you known him?
Her: About 8 or 9 months.
Me: And you don't know his name?
Her: Well shit Black, I just met his ass and he told me his name was Mark.
Me: Well actually Mark is his name (I say smiling).
Her: Dammit Black, why are you always fuckin with me!?!
Me: Cause it is so much fun! Now, empty your front right pocket for me. (She then pulls out a wadded up $10 bill and, you guessed it, her crack pipe)
Me: Turn around and let me put these bracelets on you and do not give me any trouble, do you understand me?
Her: Black you know I would never give you any trouble; you are the only Cop that treats me decent.

Me: Well I'm gonna decently arrest you so just sit down in my car and be quiet until I'm done with your buddy Mark.

I then go over and read Mark's statement, which actually turned out pretty good as far as self-written statements go. I then informed Mr. Mark of my decision. "Since you were honest with me, and since you do not have a criminal history (which I had checked on when I first made contact with him) I'm going to let you slide this time. But understand this, if I ever see you within a city block of that girl, I am going to remember this charge and I'm going to snatch your ass up so fast you will pass out from dizziness, am I clear?" "Yes sir, thank you very, very much! Can I shake your hand?" "Hell no, I know where that hand has been! Get the hell out of here before I change my mind."

I checked in route to the jail with Kelley and we had another short conversation;
Her: Black, what am I arrested for?
Me: Prostitution
Her: WHAT?!?!?!
Me: He told me that he paid you for sex.
Her: But we didn't have sex Black, you stopped us before we did it!
Me: You had enough to get you arrested Kel.
Her: You mean to tell me that I am going to jail over a $10 piece of ass?!?
Me: (laughing) Yes ma'am, that's what I'm telling you.
Her: WELL AIN'T THAT A BITCH!!!!

She sat back and didn't say anything else about her prostitution charge all the way to the jail. To this day, every single time I hear the words "Ain't that a bitch" I instantly think about her and that arrest! It makes me laugh every time.

How to start a day...

I arrived for work one morning and had just finished putting all of my gear into my patrol car getting ready for the day ahead when a call came out about an abandoned car parked on the "Turn-Around Bridge". The sun was just starting to come up as I made my way out to check on the car.

As I made the turn off of the service road to go up onto the bridge, I saw the vehicle. It was actually parked on the curving part of the road that leads up to the bridge. I couldn't see anyone around so I gave dispatch the license plate and started walking up to the car. It was not abandoned.

Inside the car were two completely naked adults, one man and one woman. They had the seats laid all the way back and were sound asleep. The way they were laying on their backs, I thought they might be dead at first, but then I noticed they were both breathing. The crack pipe and bong that were sitting on the center console between them may have had something to do with how soundly they were sleeping.

I eased back to my patrol car and called for a back-up unit and waited for his arrival before going over and rousting dumb and dumber. Looking at the passed out man, I couldn't help but puff my chest out a little bit, I didn't know they came that small on a grown man! *That's right, I got you beat sucka!*

The female was extremely blessed in the boobage department, but they're just not that attractive when one is under her left armpit and the other is under her right armpit to where they look like water floats.

My back-up officer arrived and we went to the passenger side and woke up Tiny Tim first. As soon as the door opened a bag of Cocaine fell out onto the ground. We hooked him up and then went around and woke up Miss Boobalicious. They both went to jail for possession of a controlled substance.

That's how a cop's day starts......you never know from one minute to the next what you are going to walk up on so you just ask yourself.....*What kind of crazy shit am I going to get into today?*

Good Lord he's deformed!

There's two ways to look at life, in my opinion. You can laugh at it or you can cry at it. If you are going to be a cop, you do both, but you especially better be able to laugh at whatever life decides to throw at you.

I and another officer were working one morning when we received an alarm call at an old building on the courthouse square. We both arrived at about the same time and found an open rear door. We made entry and scanned the room.

This building was one of those really old buildings that were built back in the days of saloons and whorehouses. When you walked in through the back door, the room was wide open all the way to the front of the building. There was a stairway that led to an open balcony area upstairs with rooms lined up along the balcony. *(Picture the Long Branch saloon on Gunsmoke)*

We cleared the bottom floor and made our way upstairs. The first couple of rooms were empty, so we carefully made our way down to the last room at the end of the balcony. As I tried to quietly approach the door, I could hear someone walking around inside the room.

I signaled to the other officer that someone was inside and backed back down the balcony about 20 feet. There was absolutely no place to get any cover; it was an empty building that appeared to be in the process of being remodeled. I instructed my partner to go back over to the stairwell, so that he would have a better view when the door opened. I stayed on the balcony in my position.

When we were in place, I loudly instructed whoever was in the room to open the door slowly and show me their hands. After a few seconds, the door came open and two long, skinny arms came jutting straight out of the doorway. I then told him to step out and put his hands on his head.

When this tall, skinny, pasty-white, butt-naked man stepped out of that doorway, my whole world changed. I am holding my gun straight out pointing at the man, and I'm lifting my arms so I can look under my arms to make sure I was seeing what I thought I was seeing....and I was.

This man was not a man at all.......he was only half man......from the waist down he was a damn stud horse. This son-of-a-bitch was hung past his knees and it was just swinging back and forth every time he moved! It scared me! I didn't know whether to salute his ass or shoot him!

There's not an all-male jury in the world that would have convicted me for killing this fool and getting him out of the male - female competition pool! On the other hand, every single all-female jury that's ever been would have sentenced me to death as soon as they saw the crime scene photos!

Well, come to find out, he was working on refurbishing the building and the owner had told him he could sleep in one of the rooms. After we were all finished, I and my partner were walking back to our cars, silently, and when we reach the vehicles I looked at my partner and said.... "There ain't no justice in this world" to which he replied "I know. I thought the damn thing was going to come get me!"

Ya gotta laugh or ya gotta cry……..sometimes ya gotta do both!

Difficult Story #1. The first time I had to really fight for my life

There are three stories in this book that are very difficult for me to tell. In order to truly tell a story and have people feel what you are trying to convey to them, you must re-live the situation as you are talking about it, at least in my opinion anyway. That's the only way that I know of to tell a complete, and honest, story. This is one of those stories.

It had been a long, busy day and I was exhausted and ready to go home, sit down, eat a Beef Rayford from PD's, and watch wrestling with my Aunt Sue and Uncle D. At the time, my wife and I were splitting up and I was living in an apartment behind my Aunt and Uncle's home. We used to watch wrestling together and I would sometimes stop in Terrell and grab us our favorite meal on the way home to enjoy while we screamed at the television.

I had just left the police department and was traveling down Mulberry Street, approaching Old Rail Road, when I observed an old, green-colored, Ford pickup nose down in the ditch with the rear end up in the air. There was some radio traffic going on so I pulled over to wait for the radio to clear so I could tell dispatch about the truck. At the same time, dispatch was putting out a report of a drunk driver in an old, green-colored Ford pickup that was last seen driving northbound on South Washington Street.

I was finally able to break in and tell dispatch where the truck was at when I heard someone screaming loudly. I then turned just in time to see a very tall man slam his hands down on the truck of a car as the car squealed off as fast as it could go. The car had been parked at the gas pumps of the Triple AAA Convenience Store, right next to where the truck was in the ditch.

As the car sped away, the man stumbled out into the road. One truck, and then another, nearly ran over the guy so I quickly drove over there with the intentions of getting him out of the road until an on-duty unit could arrive to handle the situation.

I was in my personal car, a small 4-door sedan, and when I pulled up to the gas station, just off East Mulberry Street, I told dispatch that I would be out on an intoxicated male and to send a unit my way. I had parked about 30 feet behind the man. I opened my door and was in the process of getting out of my car when he came running around my door with a knife in his hand.

In the next few seconds I didn't do anything, the Lord in Heaven above took over. That's the only way I can explain what happened next.

As I was getting out of my car, I had my portable radio in my left hand and my car keys in my right hand. As he came around the door of the car, he lunged at my stomach with the knife. "*I've got something for you, you motherfucking pig!*"

The next memory I have, I am lying inside my car, my left hand has a grip on his wrist and I have it pinned to the roof of my car. The knife blade is about 6 inches from my left eye. It was then that I realized I had my gun in my right hand and I had it jammed into his chest. He is screaming at me that he is going to kill me, and is doing his damndest to stab me in the face.

It is funny what kinds of things go through your mind when you are in a situation where you could die. The one thing that I thought of first was that I remembered a crowd of people standing across the street. I guess they had gathered when the incident had first started, I don't know, but I remembered they were there and was worried that if I pulled the trigger, my bullet may go through him and hit someone over there. So I pulled my gun out of his chest and placed the barrel under his chin, directly above me. I remember hating the fact that I was going to have to put a hole in the roof of my car.

Then the bad thoughts began...........
All I could see was my baby girl's face. How was I going to tell my innocent little girl that her Daddy had to kill a man?
What if my hand slips and he runs that knife through my face and neck, I could easily bleed to death and she won't have her Daddy anymore.
Will I get to hold her again?
Have I left enough insurance to take care of her?
Does she know how much I love her?

On and on these thoughts went for what seemed like an hour, but in reality was just seconds. Right then I realized that I _was_ losing my grip on his wrist. I was suddenly soaking wet with sweat, and I had to keep using all of my strength to jam his arm back against the roof of the car. Several times the knife blade was less than 2 inches from my face.

After what seemed like forever, I realized that I just couldn't hold him anymore. He had all of his weight on top of me and was continuously trying to stab me, yelling and screaming at me and I was just about spent. I thought about it briefly and accepted the fact that if it had to be him or me, then it was damn sure going to be him.

I made the decision to kill him. I said a quick prayer asking for God's forgiveness and turned my head and squinted my eyes as far closed as I could and still see, so that I didn't get his blood in my eyes. Then I started squeezing the trigger.

I was waiting for the explosion of fire, smoke and noise, it should have happened by now. But right then it came to me... I HEAR SIRENS! Suddenly I was mad. I was mad as hell! This sorry son-of-a-bitch is not going to force me to kill his coward ass. I think I can hold him off for a few more seconds. So I eased off of the trigger slowly (why didn't the damn thing fire?) and recommitted myself to keeping that knife out of my body.

I can hear people screaming.
Where are my guys?
Someone is trying to bust the window of my passenger side door.
I've got my leg up under this bastard and if they can get that knife away from him I am going to kick him so hard he will fly across Mulberry Street.
THERE'S DOUG! I can see Doug's face!
(Sergeant Doug Barker was my co-worker and best friend)
Doug is jamming his gun into the rib cage of this guy and screaming at him to drop the knife and get off of me.
I realized that Doug is screaming at this piece of shit, the piece of shit is screaming at me, and I am the only calm one in the entire bunch!

"Doug, reach in here and take that damn knife away from him, I can't hold him much longer!
(Doug is still screaming at him)
"DOUG!!!"
"Reach in here and get this fucking knife!"

(Doug had been the first Officer on scene. When he bailed out of his car, the crowd across the street started yelling and pointing towards my car. Doug thought they were pointing to an alley that was on the other side of my car so he ran that way first. When he couldn't find me, he ran back towards the street and realized that we were inside my car.)

Suddenly I see Doug's hand sliding into the car on top of the man's arm. He reaches all the way in and grabs the man's finger and starts bending and twisting them.

The only thing I can think of now is "As soon as that damn knife drops *I'm going to kick this bastards balls so hard they will bounce off his spine!"*
A little more Doug……you've almost got it buddy…….THERE IT GOES!!

I kicked. I mean I kicked with every ounce of power in my body, wanting to get this sweaty, stinking bastard off of me. I kicked so hard that I went flying out of my car! I landed on my ass on the pavement. I NEVER TOUCHED HIM! WHAT THE HELL HAPPENED?!?

I looked over and Doug and Sgt. Johnny Gilmore are on top of this man in the middle of Mulberry Street. They got him handcuffed and start pulling knife after knife out of his pockets. Suddenly someone is grabbing me and dragging me to the back of my car…..
"Where are you cut?"
"Get some bandages!"
"Did he stab you Eddie?!"
"Where's the damn ambulance!"

WAIT A MINUTE! I don't think he got me!

I looked down and I didn't see blood or intestines so I figured that was a good sign. After everything calmed down, I sorted out what had happened there at the end when I tried to kick him off of me and suddenly went airborne.

The gas station where I was attacked by a deranged man with a knife. My car was parked directly in front of the gas pump on the left. Photo by Edward Black.

The banging on my door glass was another Sergeant trying to bust out the glass with her flashlight (of course the door was locked). Right then, Sergeant Gilmore arrived. He had run up to the car and grabbed the suspect by his pants and belt and vacuumed his ass out of the car at the exact moment that I went to kick him off of me. That's why I never touched the asshole. It was all coincidental perfect timing.

When Doug was finished searching the suspect, he ran over to me, started jerking my shirt up and spinning me around looking for cuts and when he didn't find any, he just grabbed me and hugged me. Right there in front of everyone, he didn't give a damn. It's a moment I will cherish for the rest of my life.

Fast forward to trial……..

The suspect, whose name I refuse to put in my book, showed up in court in his nice new clothes that his family had, no doubt, bought him to make him look like a choir boy. He had a haircut and his facial hair was neatly trimmed. Just a perfect little model citizen.

The prosecution put me on the stand and asked me questions for about an hour. Everyone that I knew that worked at the courthouse was in the courtroom watching the trial. I was embarrassed telling the jury about the nightmares that I had been having, especially in front of my friends and coworkers. When I was finished testifying, I looked around the big room and saw almost every woman in the courtroom crying, even the women on the jury. It was a good feeling knowing that people really cared about me. When the prosecution was finished, the defense attorney stood up and stated "We have no questions for Officer Black your honor", and that was it for me on the stand.

Late in the afternoon, the jury was given the case and sent to the jury room. Me, and everyone else that had to testify, were sitting on a bench in the hallway waiting for the jury's verdict. As we were sitting there, I saw the trial judge walking down the hallway toward us. He was the longtime judge of the 86th District Court for the State of Texas and he was a Judge that you did not mess with. He ran a tight courtroom and you followed the rules. If you didn't, he had no problem stopping the proceedings and making you look like a complete fool before kicking you out of the courtroom. I had worked as his bailiff as an off-duty job one summer and I had a lot of respect for the way he took care of his business.

He walked down the hallway to where we were sitting and leaned down next to my ear. This scared the shit out of me because I thought for sure we were being too loud or had done something else wrong. He whispered "*You should have shot that son-of-a-bitch*". He stood up, patted me on the shoulder, said "Great Job Ed" and walked back down the hallway to wherever he had come from.

The suspect was convicted of Aggravated Assault on a Public Servant and sentenced to 19 years in prison and a $10,000 fine. He has since been released from the penitentiary.

I later found out that several people on the jury wanted to give him 10 years, but a single juror refused to agree to that and demanded 30 years. The others finally realized that this man meant business and was prepared to stay there as long as it took, so they compromised with 19 years. (Why 19 instead of 20, I will never know?)

I know who the lone juror was and I have thanked him personally. I would like to say "Thank You" again for standing up for Law Enforcement Officers all over the world by refusing to let this guy get off with a light sentence.

6,208 days before I had to pull the trigger

July 17, 2015 was the day that it happened to me. I was forced to pull the trigger. It's not something that I am proud of, or boast about. As a matter of fact, I never talk about it. As I write this story, I am being sued by the low-life, career criminal that tried to kill one of my officers. I haven't lost any sleep over it, whatever happens, happens, but it is a testament to how fucked up our justice system is in this day and time.

The call came in as an 18 wheeler driving around the courthouse square blowing its horn. One of the on-duty Sergeants spotted the truck and attempted to stop it, however, the idiot driving the truck decided that he would just keep driving around and blowing the horn. He was having a blast.

Several other units entered the chase and I caught up to it on South Jefferson Street, a neighborhood street where kids live and play every day. He didn't care about the kids or anything else for that matter. As he passed my car as he continued south on South Jefferson Street he was laughing and threw a beer can out the window at my car. I turned in to follow the chase and heard the lead pursuit officer say that the truck had struck a vehicle in an intersection and kept going. He didn't care if he had hurt anyone or not.

I was worried that if he kept going down Jefferson Street he would then turn back east when the road came to a dead-end at the Highway 175 service road. The service road was a one-way street going west. I was scared that he would hit another car, maybe head-on, and badly hurt or even kill someone. I made the decision to cut over to South Jackson Street and try to get down to the service road to block the east side of the intersection. I was hoping to try to force him to go west to keep him away from the crowded Washington Street corridor.

I jumped over one block to South Jackson Street and managed to beat the outlaw 18-wheeler to the service road. As I arrived, Sergeant Smith (Not his real name) also arrived. He had the same concerns that I did. We positioned our vehicles to block the service road on the east side. We had to force several vehicles to stop to keep them out of the path of the truck.

As the truck approached us, the asshole that was driving was still blowing the horn over and over again. I was standing near the front of my vehicle and drew my duty weapon, a Sig Sauer P226 .40 caliber Semi-auto. If he turned the truck and tried to run over me or Sgt. Smith, I was prepared to fire to try and stop him. He was NOT going to hurt another innocent person!

As the truck began to enter the intersection, a movement to my left drew my attention and I quickly noticed that he had caught Sgt. Smith in a bad spot. The truck was driving straight at him. I heard the engine of the truck sound like he had let off of the accelerator and thought for a split second that he was going to stop, but that belief was immediately dashed when he suddenly gunned the engine. The truck lurched forward toward Sgt. Smith as he was moving to his left. He then disappeared in front of the truck. I drew a bead and squeezed the trigger.

SMITH!

I couldn't see Smith anywhere. I knew he had been run down by the truck's cab; there was no way he could have moved out of the way fast enough. I also knew that I had hit the driver. I had a direct line of site to his shoulder and head area. Just then I realized something; I had heard other gunshots, not just my own.

The truck came to a stop at the curb of the roadway, next to the embankment that went up to the highway above. I ran around the cab of the truck and was relieved beyond words when I saw Smith. He had opened fire at the same time I had.

Suddenly, there were several officers running around the truck about to jump up onto the cab and open the door. I yelled as loud as I could....STOP, BACK AWAY, HE MAY HAVE A GUN! Everyone took a few steps back. I think I scared the shit out of them because they were so caught up in the moment they never stopped to think this guy might open fire on them.

I still had my gun pointed at the driver and noticed that he had slumped over the steering wheel and had a huge hole in the side of his head*. I told an officer to open the door and step back. He did and I could see that the driver was not going to be much of a threat at that moment. I gave the okay, and several officers pulled the wounded piece of shit out of the truck. As soon as he hit the ground I yelled for someone to call an ambulance.

I walked over to Sgt. Smith, who had sat down in the grass, and asked him if he was alright. He looked up and I could see he had been scared out of his mind. So had I. That's when I realized that I was shaking.

I later learned that Smith had tried to move to his left to get out from in front of the truck, but when the truck turned, he was caught between the cab and the trailer. He could have easily been run over and crushed to death. Sgt. Smith had fired over the front of the hood of the truck and then through the small glass window that is at the bottom of the passenger side door. That tells you how close he was to the truck.

The next couple of hours went by in a blur. The first thing I did after everything settled down was lock myself in my car and called the Texas Municipal Police Association (TMPA) and reported that I had been involved in a shooting incident. The person on the phone asked me if I was alright and then told me not to speak to anyone until I heard from my lawyer, who would be calling me in the next few minutes.

Shortly after I hung up, my phone rang just as she had said it would. The attorney asked me if I was alright and then told me he was getting in his car and would be there within the hour. He also told me not to talk to anybody until he got there. I explained to him that Sgt. Smith was also involved in the shooting. He asked me to tell him the same thing and that he would be representing both of us.

I walked over to where Smith was at and pulled him aside. I told him that I had contacted TMPA and gave him the attorney's instructions. Somewhere during this time, I directed one of my Detectives to secure the scene and collect mine and Smith's weapons for the investigation. A few minutes later the Chief of Police arrived and checked on us both. The sheriff also walked over and checked on me, as well as several other officers that I worked with throughout the community.

A little while later, the Chief came over and said that he had arranged for a Sheriff's Deputy to transport me to the police department so I could relax. He had arranged for another officer to transport Sgt. Smith.

I was later advised that the suspect was still alive and that he was going to make a full recovery. This floored me. I had seen the hole in his head; he had to be the luckiest man on the planet. It was later explained to us that the bullet had entered his scalp and travelled under the skin all the way around his head and came out under his chin. I had also shot him in his left arm, but that was not a significant injury. I was relieved that he was alive. No sane man wants to be the person to kill another human being.

Here is where this story takes a very wrong turn.

The District Attorney's Office of Kaufman County very quietly let the bastard plea to the theft of the 18 wheeler and never charged him with trying to kill Smith. We were never made aware of this until it was already done. They purposely made this deal under the table. The only way we found out about it was because we kept calling wanting to know the status of the case and a clerk finally told us what had been done.

The suspect had a criminal history that included, among many other things, his arrest for having components of explosives (the fucker was trying to build a bomb!) and they let him off with a Theft charge! It is my opinion that the reason this deal was hidden from us was because the stolen 18 wheeler happened to belong to a local attorney, who had hired the suspect to work for him, and who works in the Kaufman County Courthouse on a daily basis.

Sergeant Smith and I were beyond furious. This was not right, and there was absolutely nothing that can be done about it because the agreement was signed and sealed. We went to the Chief of Police, who contacted the District Attorney and asked for a meeting. We wanted an explanation.

The District Attorney, and her Lead Investigator, came to the Police Department and sat down with us. The bottom line, according to her, was that the deal was done without her knowledge and she apologized.

A rural county, a small courthouse, only a handful of prosecutors and the District Attorney was not involved in a decision on a case of this magnitude. You can form your own opinions. The fact that nobody lost their job because of it told me everything that I needed to know.

July 19, 2017 I am served with a summons. The criminal is now suing me and Smith. Not only does he get to walk away scot-free for trying to kill a police officer, but he gets to sue them and probably get paid a lot of money by an insurance company. I will rot in prison before that drain-on-society gets a penny from me.

Neither the Kaufman Police Department, nor the City of Kaufman, has ever recognized us for what we went through that day. Not so much as a print-your-own paper certificate. One of their officers was nearly killed trying to protect this community, and nobody saw fit to even give him a 5 cent piece of paper to say thank you. I'll leave that right there.

It was not revealed in the subsequent investigation by the Texas Rangers exactly which one of us had shot the suspect in the head. It is my opinion that I shot him in the head because the bullet had entered the suspect's head from the left side, where I was positioned. It is also my opinion that it doesn't really matter.

Crazy Woman at Circle K

The call came in as an accident. A car had driven into the gas station building. I was the Captain of the Criminal Investigations Division at that time and happened to be out driving around and was close by when the call went out, so I started that way.

As I was headed to the gas station, dispatch updated the call and stated that there was a female who had driven her car through the front of the building and was now out of the car and threatening people with a knife.......well shit.

I arrived at the location and saw that the entire front glass of the store was gone and a car was in the process of trying to back out of the building. I circled around where I had a good place for cover and jumped out of my car, gun in hand. By now the woman had freed her car from the destruction of the building and was starting to drive away.....straight at me.

I stood where I was, directly in front of the car, and had a bee-line aim at her, yelling at her to stop the car. She continued coming at me slowly at first but then started accelerating toward me. There were people everywhere, as one can imagine, and there was no way I could safely fire at her so I jumped out of the way and she drove by me, missing me by inches.

As I entered my car I could hear on the radio the Constable of Precinct 1 in Kaufman County, Shawn Mayfield, telling all of the other units that she tried to run me over. He had just pulled in when she drove by me, so he fell in behind her in pursuit. I followed him and several other units were arriving in the area about the same time.

The pursuit didn't last long, or go very far, before she tried to make a turn but the car's tires slid in some gravel that was on the roadway and she came to a stop pinned between Constable Mayfield and a large Coca-Cola truck. I bailed out and was standing at the driver's door with my gun pointed at her. If she came up with a knife or any other weapon, she was dead. The door was locked so someone busted out the door glass. Another officer was standing there, and as soon as that glass shattered, that bitch rode-lightening. That's what it feels like when you get Tased with 50,000 volts of electricity.

We managed to get her out of the car and handcuffed without any officers getting hurt, other than a few cuts from the broken glass. We were still in the process of trying to figure out what the hell just happened when someone who knew her told me that she has kids at home.

I directed officers to her residence just a few blocks away and told them they had permission to force entry if they needed to. A short time later the officers called for the fire department at the house. She had tried to burn it down but, thank God, there were no kids in the house. They were visiting their grandmother at the time.

The suspect was found to be on drugs and was later sentenced to spend several years in the state penitentiary. Unbelievably, nobody had been injured when she drove her car into the building.

The front of the Circle K after a woman intentionally crashed her car into the front of the building. She then tried to run over me.
Photo Credit: inForney.com

Mr. Bacon has been robbed again.

Bacon Lumber was a fixture of Kaufman. Located on East Mulberry Street it was a tall, light colored building with a small parking lot out front. Outside the front of the building was a neat, clean place, but inside it looked like a bomb went off, and that was normal operating procedures!

The building was jam-packed with everything from nails and screws to antique knick-knacks. Mr. Bacon had things crammed in every crook and crevice in the store, but if you walked in and told him you needed something, he knew exactly where to find it.

Mr. Bacon was a small man and up in years. He had been robbed at his store multiple times and kept a small pistol on him most of the time. He had no enemies, but he was an easy target for low-life scum looking for a free hand-out any way they could get it.

The Ethridge family of Kaufman seemed to enjoy robbing and assaulting Mr. Bacon. In one instance, one of the Ethridge boys had tried to hold up Mr. Bacon and he earned a bullet for it. Score one for the good guys!

I was in Grapevine, Texas attending training and was on my way back to Kaufman after a long day in class. I turned on the police radio and heard the officers talking about a robbery at Bacon Lumber. They were calling for an ambulance. The elderly gentleman had been hurt and hurt bad.

At the hospital they discovered that Mr. Bacon had been struck in the head with something so hard that his ear had almost been ripped completely off. He had been beaten by a coward that we later learned was almost a foot and a half taller than he was and about 30 years younger.

The prime suspect was one of the Ethridge boys....again. This time it was Ricky Ethridge. Ricky had a drug problem and needed quick cash for his next fix. He decided to nearly kill a senior citizen to get it.

The next morning was Saturday and I was on duty along with a newly hired officer. As the sun came up, I decided to go walk the neighborhood streets behind Bacon Lumber to see if I could get lucky and spot any evidence of the offense. A witness had seen the suspect run behind the store before losing sight of him.

A heavy dew had settled on the grass that morning. It was a little foggy and there was very little traffic on Grove Street, where I was searching the ditches for anything that looked out of place, having no clue what that might be. I had walked about three blocks and didn't want to get too far from my car, so as I was about to turn around and head back, I spotted something that seemed out of place.

In the front yard of a vacant, small, brick house I noticed what looked like a t-shirt or sweatshirt lying just inside the chain-link fence on the grass. I'm not sure why it caught my eye, maybe it looked too new to be laying on the ground in the yard of a vacant house, maybe I had seen it before, and maybe God just said "Hey Ed, go look at that". I will never know why, but it turned out to be the nail in Ethridges' coffin.

I went over to the gate of the fenced-in yard, which was standing open. It was very apparent that the house was vacant and had been for a while, so there was nobody that I could speak to and ask for permission to enter the yard and look at the item. Therefore, I believed it to be abandoned property, meaning I didn't need a warrant.

I walked into the yard and put on my gloves. As I slowly lifted the item from the ground, I noticed that the grass underneath was not dead or dying, telling me that the item had not been there very long at all. The shirt was wet from the heavy dew, meaning it had been there all night. This information led me to believe that it was something I definitely needed to collect and show to the Investigators. I slowly unfolded the wadded up shirt, which was green and blue. Then I noticed the dark brown stains all over the front of the shirt……*that could be blood!*

I called the other officer on the radio and told him to bring me a paper bag out of my squad car. I placed the shirt into the bag and carried it back to my car. At the station, I filled out the chain-of-custody tag and placed the shirt over a rope that I had tied up across the room so that the shirt would dry. We did not have any of those fancy drying cabinets like other Police Departments so we had to make do. I filled out my report and placed a copy in the Investigators' door tray so she would see it first thing Monday morning.

Monday afternoon I was called to the CID (Criminal Investigations Division) office. As I walked in, the Investigator jumped up and hugged me! *"You are awesome Eddie!"* She told me that she had shown the shirt to the witness, who verified that it was the shirt that Ethridge was wearing when he had robbed Mr. Bacon. I was about to bust wide-open with the pride that I was feeling at that moment.

The shirt was sent to the state crime lab for testing the dark brown stains. The report came back.....it was blood. Not only was it blood, but it was BOTH Mr. Bacon's and Ethridges' blood! *Turn out the lights, the parties over Mr. Ethridge!*

At trial, I was called to the witness stand by the prosecution to tell the story to the jury of how I found the shirt. When the state was finished, the defense attorney came at me. She was a tall, thin, small-framed woman with long brown hair that came down almost to her waist. She didn't look like any defense attorney that I had ever done battle with before.

She kept harping on the fact that I didn't wait to get a search warrant to go into the yard and, therefore, the evidence was collected illegally. She kept asking me the same questions over and over again, and I could tell that she was getting irritated that my answers were very short and to the point.

"So you saw this shirt inside the fenced yard correct?"
"Yes Ma'am"
"And you didn't think you needed a warrant to enter that fenced-in yard"
"No ma'am"
"Was the gate closed?"
"No ma'am"
"How far open was it?"
"Open far enough for me to walk through without touching it"
"Why didn't you try to find the owner of the house to get permission?"
"I didn't need to Ma'am"
"You didn't need to? Why not Officer Black?"

"Because it was a vacant residence, therefore, I believed the property was abandoned"
"No further questions your honor"

That is how the back and forth went for about a half hour. After the trial was over and the low-life coward was sentenced to a very long time in the state penitentiary, the defense attorney came up to me outside the courthouse and shook my hand.
"I don't know who taught you how to testify Officer Black, but they should teach a class! You wouldn't give me anything to work with!"
"Thank you Ma'am"

Mr. Bacon did recover from this attack, but his health rapidly declined after that. He was one tough old boy!

Today, there stands a Dollar General on the spot where Bacon Lumber used to be located. Just what Kaufman needed, another damned dollar store.

Largest drug find of my career

Here's some free advice for all of you dope dealers out there....write it down.......are you ready.......*DON'T BRING ATTENTION UPON YOURSELF WHEN YOU ARE HAULING YOUR PRODUCT!*

Most drug arrests occur during traffic stops. Simple traffic violations like a taillight out, or speeding, is what gets most drug couriers caught. But a pissed off woman will get you caught every time!

I was dispatched to a call of a "rolling domestic" or a domestic disturbance in a moving vehicle for all you non-police folks. The caller stated that there was a man and woman in a Maroon Chevy Camaro and they were coming into Kaufman on Highway 34 from Terrell. The caller last saw the vehicle turning right onto West Mulberry Street.

I was close to the area but could not find the car. There is usually a short delay between the caller telling our dispatchers something and them getting that information to us, so this happens frequently. I was not busy at the time so I continued looking for the car around the northern part of town.

I made my way over to the courthouse square and when I came around the corner, there sat a Maroon Camaro with a man and woman inside arguing. I eased up behind the vehicle and hit my red and blue flashing lights. The man instantly jumped out of the driver's seat and started walking to the sidewalk. I told him to stand where he was and keep his hands where I could see them. He started telling me that he was late for court and he really needed to get to the courthouse.

I patted him down and just as I was finishing, his attorney came walking down the sidewalk. He was a real sorry bastard that I had heard nothing but bad things about. He approached and asked if he could get his client to the courthouse because the judge was waiting. After identifying the man, and the attorney, I told him he could go to the courthouse (what can I say, I was young and dumb!).

I then walked over to the passenger side of the car to speak to the woman. She rolled the window down approximately 1 inch when I asked her to roll it down. RED FLAG! I told her to step out of the car, but she initially refused to do so. I told her to get her ass out of the car or I would remove her from it. She then opened the door, stepped out, and quickly locked and shut the door.

I got her information and ran her and the man over the radio to dispatch for a warrant check. As soon as I was finished giving the information, my Lieutenant got on the radio and asked if I was familiar with the man. I told him that I was not and he stated that he would be at my location shortly. *SHIT, I LET HIM GO TO THE COURTHOUSE!*

The Lieutenant arrived and informed me that the man that I had let walk away was one of the largest, most prolific dope dealers in Kaufman County. I told him what was going on, and about the woman not wanting me near the car. At that time, a Kaufman County K9 Deputy arrived on scene. He had heard the name over the radio as well and immediately knew he wanted to run his K9 around the car I had stopped.

I asked the woman for consent to search the car and she flat refused. That was expected, so now we let the 4-legged officer have his turn. The dog went absolutely bat-shit crazy on the car! That gave me probable cause to search the vehicle and when I opened the door; the smell of Ether slapped me in the face so hard I nearly fell down. I had never smelled it that strong before.

There was a black bag in the floorboard where the woman had been sitting. I picked it up and opened it and pulled out a gallon size zip-lock baggie that was half full of freshly cooked, still warm Methamphetamine! I told the Lieutenant and Deputy to watch her and I sprinted to the courthouse as fast as a fat man could! I went upstairs to the District Court where the attorney had told me they were going.

As I approached the courtroom, the hallway was packed with people. Just as I was about to enter the courtroom to see if I had been lied to, out walks the man and his lawyer with big smiles on their faces. That didn't last long. I stood directly in front of the fat, bearded attorney and told him, "I'm here to arrest your client, get out of my way". I then grabbed the suspect and had him handcuffed before he knew what hit him.

The lawyer tells me "Wait just a minute" and I tell him to be quiet. I was in the process of searching the suspect when he looked at the lawyer and says "Take my wallet and give it to so and so" I said hold up. I grabbed and opened the wallet to find that there was a bunch of cash inside. "That belongs to me bud" I said as I start walking the dope-dealing shithead through the crowd and out to the car.

As I round the corner of the building and start walking my prisoner down the sidewalk with his attorney two steps behind, the K9 Deputy looks up and says "Oh now I know why he is driving around with so much Meth, he had to pay his crooked ass attorney with it!" I looked over at the deputy and I could immediately tell that he and the lawyer had a history.

"That's nice; a piece of shit dope dealer has a piece of shit lawyer to represent him!" I was thoroughly entertained by the deputy unloading on the scumbag litigator.

Inside the car I also found a bullet-proof vest, which was very illegal for the convicted felon to possess, a butt-load of drug paraphernalia, and drug dealer tools of the trade like scales, baggies, etc.

I seized the doper's Camaro and sent both him and his girlfriend to prison, but before he was sentenced, the suspect had two more encounters with the law, both with him hauling dope, both which resulted in him losing sports cars! I was told that the feds finally came in and seized all of his property and sent him away for a good long while to see if he could figure out the error of his ways.

The meth that I seized that day weighed 243 grams. The largest piece inside the bag was as big as a softball! As of the writing of this story, that amount has not been beaten by any officer of the department.

And I've never let anyone leave one of my scenes again until I was finished with my business!

Difficult Story #2-The Murder Case of Kelley Osgan

"I recognize her shoes, it's Kelley Osgan".

Those were my words as I stood in the thick patch of trees staring at the legs and feet of a body that were sticking out from under a blue colored, go-cart frame. The frame was sitting on a concrete slab that was the foundation of a long ago demolished railroad building. The go-cart frame was designed to look like a Formula 1 race car and an old couch cushion had been stuffed down into the frame, over the body. There were broken crack pipes, beer cans, and trash all over the ground.

It was a spot the locals called "The Trees" and was where the neighborhood tweakers would go to smoke their drugs and drink their beer. Located inside a large clump of trees and shrubs on some property that was still owned by the railroad, the spot was also a place for prostitutes to take their johns. Used condoms were strewn about. The location was on the north side of town between East First North Street and Grove Street. A nice little hiding spot in the middle of a neighborhood.

On the morning of August 9th 2006, an employee of the local Ford dealership, Todd Jackson*, was approached by a local boozer, who he sometimes gave a few dollars to. The man told him that he had heard there was a dead body in "the trees". He continued that he had went over there to see if people were telling the truth and there was a horrible smell so he didn't go up into the bushes. That had been the day before.

Jackson decided he had better call the police department and report what the man had told him, just in case there was something to it. A Kaufman Police Department Sergeant arrived at the dealership, and he explained to the officer what he was told. The officer and Jackson then drove a couple of blocks down the street to the location indicated. When they opened the doors of the car, they both immediately smelled the stench of decaying flesh.

The Sergeant on-scene went about making his way into the foliage as Jackson politely declined to accompany him. He immediately noticed the legs and feet of a body and backed out of the trees and started stringing yellow Crime Scene tape around the area after calling for Investigators.

I, along with my partner and several other employees, was sitting down to eat at a local Mexican food place called "La Fuentes" when I received a telephone call from Dispatch. She informed me that a body had been located and told me where. Just as the waiter sat my plate down in front of me, I got up and left. It was a scene repeated many times over my career.

Upon arrival, I did not like where he had placed the barrier of the crime scene, so I directed him to tape off an area twice the size of what he had already done. My Lieutenant had arrived on scene, as well as a couple of more officers. The first thing we had to do was get permission from the railroad to go onto their property to work our crime scene. Our department's Dispatcher who was on-duty at the time was named Connie Davis. I called her and told her I needed a contact with Union Pacific Railroad, who had the authority to provide legal authorization to go on their property and I needed it fast.

About 15 minutes later, she called and gave me a telephone number and told me that they were waiting for my call. When the man answered the phone, I told him who I was and he told me that we had permission from Union Pacific Railroad to do anything we needed to do, for as long as we needed to do it. He also told me that he was faxing over an authorization letter that gave the Kaufman Police Department legal access to the property from that day forward.

The place the locals called "The Trees" where the body of Kelley Osgan was discovered.
Photo by Edward Black

I, along with my partner Sergeant Doug Barker, made our way into the thick bushes and over to where we were told the body was located. I noticed the blue jeans were grungy and dirty, but the tennis shoes were clean and white. *"I recognize her shoes, it's Kelley Osgan".* Doug agreed with me. She always kept her shoes clean and white; I guess it was a quirk of hers. Of course, we still had to verify the identity of the corpse.

Her blue-jeans were pulled down around her knees that much we could tell before moving anything. We stepped back out to the vehicles and grabbed handfuls of paper bags and other evidence collection tools, along with a camera. We then went back in and began the gruesome task of collecting evidence. We were assisted by the Kaufman County Sheriff Department's Crime Scene Unit while processing the scene.

The blue-colored, Formula 1 style go-cart frame was placed over her body by her killer. He had stuffed a seat cushion from an old couch that was discarded nearby, down on top of her body, inside the frame. He probably didn't know it, but the killer had just built an oven where his victim's body would cook in the 100-plus degree weather for the next several days.

We slowly and carefully removed the seat cushion from the frame of the go-cart and placed it into an evidence bag. Under the cushion we observed a large piece of concrete that had been placed over her head and face. We lifted the heavy piece of concrete off of her and set it aside to be collected. Her face was gone; there would be no visual identification. Her shirt had been pulled up above her breasts and a 40 ounce bottle of Natural Light beer had been placed between her legs, on top of her vaginal area.

We photographed each step of the way to document the process. We lifted the go-cart frame off of her and set it aside on some large paper bags. The body had simply baked in the oppressive August heat. There was absolutely no way to tell who it was definitively, or we didn't think so.

Texas Ranger Richard Shing arrived on scene to help us. I was sure glad he did because my experienced Lieutenant was not interested in the least bit in helping us. I was pretty pissed about that at the time, but I had a job to do so I put my anger aside. Did I mention that this was my very first Homicide investigation?

It was time to turn the body over and have a look at her backside for any clues. With the Ranger's help, we slowly rolled the body over. Doug spotted a small tattoo, barely visible, on her upper left shoulder blade. We took a picture of it and laid her back down. I immediately called for an officer to go to the station and bring me booking photos of Kelley Osgan.

When we were finished processing the scene, we retrieved a body bag from the funeral home personnel. They were waiting to collect the body for transport to the Dallas County Medical Examiner's Office for an autopsy. As we were attempting to lift the body and place it in the bag, her head suddenly rolled away on the ground! The Texas Ranger, without missing a beat, said, "Now don't lose your head Kelley". You have to laugh while doing this kind of work or you'll lose your mind. Some people take it to mean cops are cold-blooded, or we don't care about the victims, when they see us being light-hearted at crime scenes, but the truth is, it's the exact opposite. We have to maintain our sanity in order to bring justice to the victims and their families.

As we came out of the trees with the body and placed it into the van, a Patrol Officer walked up and handed me the photos that I had called for. There it was, the tattoo. It was definitely Kelley. The first question that came to my mind was "Where is Lenny?" It didn't take long to find him; he was locked up in the Kaufman County Jail and had been for over a month. This was going to be harder than I thought.

In Dallas, the Medical Examiner could only speculate about the cause of death because the body was in such bad shape. The "Hyoid" bone was missing from the body, which is a bone in the throat that could help the Medical Examiner decide if a person had been strangled to death. His final speculation was that she had been beaten severely about the face, neck, and head area and was most likely strangled. Her death was ruled "Death by homicidal violence", based more on the crime scene than anything from the body. We didn't get much help from the autopsy results.

Tips started coming in from every direction. She was killed by two Mexican men in a van. She was killed by a john from Terrell; she was killed by Lenny, and on and on. Our first big break came when we learned that while Lenny had been locked up, Kelley had hooked up with a man named Rodney "Rondale" Hunt and had been staying with him at his mom's house. The word on the street was that they fought all the time.

Soon after we started looking for Rondale, we were contacted by a clerk at a Dollar Store on the north side of town. She asked for an Investigator to come speak with her. Later that day, Doug went to see her. She gave us information that pointed us to some big pieces of the puzzle.

The clerk stated that at the end of July, Rondale came into the store and purchased a romantic card and a small stuffed tiger. When she asked him who he was buying the gift for, he stated "Kelley". The clerk then watched him write S.W.A.K. (Sealed with a kiss) on the outside of the envelope and then left. The clerk went on to state that on Friday, August 4th; Rondale came into the store and was visibly upset. When the clerk asked him what was wrong, he stated that he and his mother had been fighting.

She told us that Rondale asked if he could borrow some money for a bus ticket to go to his sister's house in Huntsville. (We later assisted him in getting to Huntsville, but not exactly the way he had wanted). The clerk stated that Rondale told her that he had to "get the hell out of here".

The next day, we tracked down Rondale. He claims that he hadn't seen Kelley since July 31st at his residence. He stated that she got mad at him and went to Terrell and that he hadn't seen her since. I asked him if he would agree to take a polygraph and he agreed.

The next day we transported Rondale to the Mesquite Police Department where he promptly bombed the polygraph. While I, and Ranger Shing, was interviewing him after the failed polygraph, Rodney Hunt admitted that he had killed Kelley Osgan. We transported him back to Kaufman where I was going to interview him and take his statement. On the way back to Kaufman, the ride was just as laid back as it had been on the way to Mesquite. Not one word was said about the case the entire trip.

When we got back to the police department, Rondale asked if he could go outside and smoke. At that time, he was not in custody and could leave at any time he wanted to. I told him he certainly could and had another officer go outside with him while he sucked down some cancer. If he decided to leave I wanted to make sure we kept eyes on him until I could obtain a warrant.

A few minutes later, I was called outside. Rondale was suddenly having the fakest damn seizure I've ever seen. It was funny as hell watching him act so pitiful. I told the dispatcher to send an ambulance to check him out. While being examined by the paramedic, Rondale made the statement "I'm fine, just really nervous because I'm confessing to a murder". After EMS examined him and found absolutely nothing wrong with him, I asked Rondale if he wanted to go to the hospital, go home or would he still come inside and talk to me. The dumb son-of-a-bitch agreed to come inside and let me interview him!

Once inside, and after I advised him of his Miranda rights, Rodney Lamont Hunt confessed that he had beaten Kelley unconscious. He went on to describe climbing on top of her after she had fallen to the ground and pounding on her face and head repeatedly. He told us that he had left her lying there. He then admitted to placing the cement block on her head, then the couch cushion, and then the go-cart frame. He denied ever placing the beer bottle between her legs, who knows why. He even apologized to a picture of Kelley for what he had done to her.

On October 11, 2007, in the 86th District Court of the State of Texas, Rodney Lamont Hunt was convicted of First Degree Murder and sentenced to 99 years in the Institutional Division of the Texas Department of Criminal Justice. He was also ordered to pay a $10,000 fine.

Hunt has filed appeal after appeal in this case claiming, among other things, that when he spoke to Ranger Shing and I at the Mesquite Police Department, that we obtained a false confession because we did not advise him of his Miranda Rights. Time and again, the Appeals Courts have affirmed his conviction. What it all boils down to is one, single, solitary question that I asked Rondale on the day of his confession.....After his fake seizure, I asked him if he wanted to go to the hospital, go home, or did he want to come inside and speak to me.

 My asking that single question is the only reason that Hunt is serving his life behind bars. Every appellate court has stated in their briefs that when I asked him that question, it proved that he was not in custody and I was not forcing him to confess to me. The other item that each Appellate court has mentioned is that I never referred back to the interview in Mesquite while I was interviewing him at the station. If I had done so, the courts have stated, then his second confession would have been "tainted" and thrown out.

I tell you this to show you that no matter how well a Police Officer, Detective, or Investigator does their job, all it takes sometimes is one question, or sentence, or one small act that can set a suspect free. *Think about that for a minute.*

During the years that I knew her, I tried many times to help Kelley Michelle Osgan find her way to sobriety, it just wasn't meant to be for her I guess. You can't help someone that refuses to help themselves, but that doesn't mean it doesn't bother you. I've been able to help several people get off of drugs during my career, but Kelley was hell bent on dying young.

Rodney Hunt is currently serving his time at the Stiles Unit in Beaumont, Texas. He continues to file appeals.

Newspaper clipping of me escorting Rodney Lamont Hunt from the Kaufman Police Department as we transported him to the Kaufman County Jail for booking.

The Standoff on Main Street

Getting shot at makes me angry. Getting shot at in the middle of the night, for hours, just plain pisses me off! That's exactly what took place during the early morning hours of January 25, 2016.

I was sound asleep all snug in my bed at home dreaming about Carrie Underwood when right around midnight the phone began to scream at me. I took a second to get my bearings and answered the call.
"Captain Black, we have a standoff in progress in the 1300 block of Main Street and shots have been fired and the guy is still shooting at officers".

Well shit, Carrie I'll have to catch you later.

The caller was one of our dispatchers named Kandice and she knew exactly what information to give me before I even had to ask for it. She is one of the best I've ever been blessed to work with. "I'll be there as soon as I can" I said as I hung up and rolled out of bed at the same time. My sleepy wife, Leslie, had her standard admonishment when this happened, never even rolling over....."*Be safe Edward Glen!"*

We won't discuss how fast I drove, but 27 minutes later I was parked at the taped off perimeter of the scene. I wanted to lay eyes on my officers before anything else happened. After I made sure that my guys were all okay, I stopped long enough so that everybody who needed to speak to me got their chance. I answered all of their questions, and then started asking mine. I was advised that the gunman had already shot his son, who had been taken to the hospital. I later learned that the son suffered a gunshot wound to his hand and was released from the hospital before the end of this incident.

One of my officers, along with a KSO Deputy was pinned down behind a car in the driveway of the residence where this asshole was firing rounds at them. I wanted them out of there and replaced with Tactical Officers who had more fire power. I grabbed the Kaufman County Sheriff Department S.W.A.T. Team Commander and told him what I wanted done. He promptly put in motion the plan to make it happen and in about

15 minutes I was escorting our officer to his patrol vehicle and sending him to the station to relax and catch his breath.

Every so often the prick inside the house would randomly fire off rounds, causing everyone to drop behind whatever they happened to be near. I instructed one of my officers to notify dispatch every time the idiot fired a round. Here is that list;

12:58 a.m. - 1 shot
2:06 a.m. - 5 shots
2:17 a.m. - 2 shots
2:40 a.m. - 1 shot
2:43 a.m. - 6 shots
2:46 a.m. - 1 shot (hit a propane tank in his garage causing it to spew propane into the air)
2:56 a.m. - 1 shot
2:57 a.m. - 3 shots
3:06 a.m. - 1 shot
4:10 a.m. - 1 shot
4:16 a.m. - 5 shots
6:10 a.m. - 1 shot

The suspect inside the house was identified as Michael Etheredge (Not the same Ethridge family discussed in another story). After he shot the propane tank trying to make it explode, I decided that it was too dangerous to leave the family next door inside their home. The officers had made contact with them earlier and told them to stay in the farthest bedroom away from the house where we were at, but now that he was trying to cause an explosion, I knew there was no telling what this shithead would do and we needed to evacuate them.

Michael Etheredge being taken into custody and me addressing the media. Photo credit Fox 4 DFW.

I took another officer and made my way up to the door. When they answered I told them that we needed to get them out of there. The man and woman gathered up their children and I gave them some last minute instructions. "*Stay directly behind me. If you hear gunshots, drop to the ground and lay flat. Do not move until I tell you to."*

I led them out and directly south, away from the suspect's house. I asked them if they had any family or friends where they could go and they told me that they had family but they were an hour away. They also informed me that they had just moved to Kaufman a couple of weeks ago and didn't really know anyone yet. The lady then said that she had been talking to the woman who lived across the street from them and she believed that she would let them stay at her house until their family arrived to pick them up.

I had a decision to make. I had no vehicles that I could get them to safely and it was freezing outside. The kids couldn't stay out in the cold, half asleep and scared. I decided to take them to the neighbor's house that was located across the street and just to the south of the scene.

We made our way across the street and back up to the front door of the friendly neighbor. Just as we were approaching the front porch a shot rang out. The family did exactly like I had told them and dropped to the ground. I jumped over them and crouched down in front of the woman and her smallest child. When no other shots were fired I knocked on the front door and the lady inside quickly opened the door and welcomed the family into her home.

My next problem came to me a short time later......*School buses.* It was a school day and the buses would start running pretty soon. I telephoned the Kaufman I.S.D. Police Chief and advised her of the situation. I told her to keep all school buses out of the area until this thing was resolved. I then directed officers to go to every house in the immediate neighborhood and tell each family to keep their kids inside until further notice. We were within 1000 feet of Phillips Elementary School as the crow flies and that concerned me greatly. I made another call to the K.I.S.D. Police Chief and asked them to suspend classes at the school until we were finished dealing with this psycho. To their credit, they never hesitated for a second in granting my request.

The S.W.A.T. Commander advised me that he had requested the assistance of the Mesquite Police Department's Tactical Unit and their armored vehicle. The giant truck arrived within the hour and the two teams devised their plan. A hostage negotiator had already been working to establish a dialogue with Yosemite Sam without much success.

At 8:11 a.m. the gunman walked out and gave himself up without incident. He was arrested and removed from the scene in seconds. It was then my responsibility to go address the media that had been set up about 3 blocks down the street. When I had finished answering all of their questions, I headed back to the office. I sat down and did what I do every time there is a major incident; I reviewed the department policy regarding that type of situation to make sure we did everything correctly. We had.

Online News article after Etheredge was sentenced. Photo credit inForney.com

Michael W. Etheredge was charged with 2 counts of Aggravated Assault against a Public Servant. He pled guilty to one count and was found guilty by a jury on the second. On October 20, 2016 he was sentenced to 30 years in prison and on November 10th he was sentenced to 20 more years in prison. He will be eligible for parole on January 23, 2031. He currently resides at the Telford Unit in New Boston, Texas.

The Hardest Story to Tell

There has not been many cases throughout my career that I feel have permanently affected me, this is definitely one of those that did and is an extremely difficult story for me to talk about. I almost didn't put it in this book, but after thinking about it for a while, I decided it is too much a part of me not to. If I want to be honest to whoever decides to read this book, then I can't hide the worst days of my career from them. So here goes.

This story is dedicated to Kelly and Chyanne

It was a beautiful February day and I was out patrolling the neighborhoods as usual. I traveled south down South Dallas Street, made a loop through the "Old Folks Apartments" as they were known then, circled back around and started heading west on East Fifth Street. I saw Lenny in his front yard washing his tractor-trailer cab in the driveway. I stopped rolled down the passenger side window and said hello. He yelled back and asked if I wanted to finish washing the truck for him. I told him I would be back later though so he could wash my squad car. We both laughed and I was on my way to finish my patrols. Little did I know that in a few hours he was going to murder his wife and 9 year old daughter inside the house.

I used to see Lenny Gallien a couple of times a week at the 7-Eleven store. He would always stop in there for coffee and scratch off tickets. He was always pleasant to me and we often joked and cut up when I stepped in to grab a Dr. Pepper and he was in there.

February 19, 2002 started out like any other day in a small town cop's life. I caught up on the prior shift's activity and hit the street. A couple of hours later, I was called to the police department by the Lieutenant. It seems a local pastor had received a call from one of his church members stating that he had killed his wife and daughter in their home. We had to go check it out. We then headed to the 500 block of East Fifth Street.

"It just can't be true Lieutenant; I just talked with Lenny yesterday, right here in this driveway."

All of the doors and windows were locked so we had to break a window and sent in a skinny cop to climb through and open the front door. He did and we made entry silently.

We cleared the kitchen, living room, and bathroom and then started to the bedrooms, where we were praying to God that Gallien was lying. I took the bedroom at the end of the hall on the left and the Lieutenant took the one on the right. I had drawn the short straw.

I opened the door and stepped inside the room. There was a dresser immediately on the right and a large bed, between the two lay the body of Kelly. I knew then that the baby was dead also and was praying over and over that I didn't have to find her. Across the room and to the left was a bathroom door that was closed. I had to clear that room before I could do anything else. For all we knew, Lenny could be inside there with a gun.

I started slowly making my way across the room and on the other side of the bed, on the floor, was the baby. She was almost the exact same age as my daughter Chelsea.

That's all I'm going to say about that.

We finished clearing the house and backed out to obtain a search warrant. Now we had to find the coward that had done this. He had told his pastor that he was heading "back home" to Louisiana and was going to kill himself. We never believed that for a second. If he had intended to kill himself he would have done it right there in that room.

We put out an "Attempt to Locate" on his White Ford Expedition, and on February 20, 2002, the next day, a Patrol Officer with the Oklahoma City Police Department was doing random checks of vehicle license plates in the parking lot of the Rockwell Inn, a motel on the west side of Oklahoma City, when he got a hit. The vehicle belonged to a Capital Murder suspect out of Kaufman, Texas.

At about 2:30 a.m. the Oklahoma City Police surrounded the motel and called the room that the suspect had rented. They told him straight out that he was surrounded and there was no way he would escape. Lenny Gallien slowly walked out of his motel room and was taken into custody.

The Lieutenant working the case, and a Texas Ranger immediately left for Oklahoma City to try and interview Gallien. He ended up confessing to killing Kelly because they were arguing and she "allegedly" told him that the little girl was not his. He says he then went to the side of the bed and called the child in there to him and then he said "she just looked down, she knew what was coming".

On November 26, 2003, 645 days after he destroyed the lives of so many people, Larry Lynn Gallien was sentenced to life in prison. He is eligible for Parole on February 19, 2032.
There was a lot of controversy surrounding the prosecution of Gallien. The District Attorney at the time was a CIVIL attorney who had been elected to run the CRIMINAL District Attorney's office and was rumored to be incompetent in the courtroom.

He worked a deal with Gallien where he did not have to go to trial and face the death penalty. The DA came out and publicly stated that the family of Kelly and Chyanne had asked him not to pursue the death penalty. The family later declared this to be an outright lie.

I have never described to any living person what I saw in that bedroom that morning in 2002, and I never will. That's between me and the Lord above.

The family of Kelly and Chyanne were incredibly strong throughout this ordeal and handled themselves with more class than anyone had a right to ask for. I hope and pray that somehow time has minimized their pain, though I know it will never leave them.

It has never left me.

The house where Kelly and Chyanne were killed as it looks today. Photo by Edward Black.

Pit Bulls Suck!

In 2016, there were 41 U.S. dog bite-related fatalities. Pit bulls accounted for more than half of those (22)*. During my career, every serious dog bite call that I am aware of, on people or animals, has involved Pit Bulls. While I personally would never own a Pit Bull, I am not interested in getting into a heated debate with anyone over this issue. I call it like I see it.

Miss Dorthy Hamilton was a tiny, frail, little elderly woman and on March 31, 2014 she was left at home alone with her son's six, large aggressive Pit Bulls. Two of the largest animals were kept in his bedroom. Her son had warned his mother to never go in that room and never open the door. He *knew* they were dangerous animals.

I was on my mower cutting the lawn when my wife walked out and signaled to me that I had a telephone call. I knew that if she was coming out to get me that it must be important so I wheeled over to the garage and took the phone from her. My Investigator had a solemn tone in his voice. *"It's bad Captain, they chewed on this poor woman"*. I got cleaned up and headed to Kaufman thinking about, and preparing myself, for what I was going to see when I got on scene. It's just something that you learn to do.

When I arrived at the scene, there were already large crowds gathered in every direction. I went to the rear of the Crime Scene Van and began suiting up. We had to put on full protective body suits because there was so much blood and flesh all over the place. I instructed one of the officers on scene to find some barriers of some kind, so that when we bring the body out we could shield it from the Social Media posting gawkers.

As I walked inside, I almost couldn't believe what I saw. They were hoarders. The house was stacked so full of junk that one could only walk through the house on the narrow "trails" that they had made for themselves. Miss Dorthy was lying on the floor in the living room in a giant pool of blood. Parts of her had been eaten by the dogs and other parts were scattered around the room. Four feet from her body was the bedroom door with a hole busted through the bottom of it. There had been a small hole about the size of a softball in the door and her son had placed a piece of plywood over it to keep the dogs from chewing their way out of the room. It didn't work.

The house on East First North Street where 86 year old Dorthy Hamilton was killed by her son's pit bulldogs.
Photo by Edward Black.

The dogs had managed to pull the piece of wood down and bust through the door to get at her. She never had a chance once they escaped the bedroom. Her son was at work when a neighbor had called him to tell him his dogs were fighting and that he needed to come home and do something about them. When he arrived at the house, he discovered his mother's body. As I observed him at the scene, he appeared more "bothered" than devastated that his mom had been savagely killed by his pets.

After processing the scene and collecting evidence, we prepared a case against the victim's son and presented it to the District Attorney. The only thing the ADA assigned to the case cared about was trying to prove the son was involved in organized dog fighting. He wasn't, at all. We were called numerous times by the ADA wanting us to look at this dog fighting ring, or that dog fighting characteristic. He refused to listen to us that the man was not involved in any dog fighting activity. We tried to explain to them that he actually loved his dogs.

I ultimately sent word to the DA's office, that we would not waste any more time trying to prove a link to a dog fighting ring, we were finished. The case ultimately went nowhere. We got a court order to have the dogs destroyed and that was the end of it. The victim's son never had to take any responsibility for his mother's horrible death.

I am told that today, he still keeps Pit Bulls as pets.

*According to CanineJournal.com

If that's not a bag of dope I'll salute you!

I was an FTO (Field Training Officer) for the department when I was assigned to train a man that later became my best friend. Doug Barker was pretty timid when I was training him. He had worked for the Kemp Police Department before coming to work for us, but down there he was given a ticket book and told to go write as many tickets as he could. He wasn't provided with the training that every police officer on earth needs and deserves. He may have been timid at first, but it didn't take long to realize that he was the funniest son-of-a-bitch I have ever met!

We were out training one day when we were dispatched to some apartments on Cates Drive to meet with the manager. When we arrived, the manager met us at the street, pointed at an upstairs apartment and said "they are smoking weed in that apartment right now".

Well alrighty then!

I looked at Doug and asked him "What are you gonna do?"
Ummm, well, we can't really just go busting in there because the manager says they are smoking weed in there can we?
Nope.
We could get CID over here and see if they can get us a search warrant...?
What is your probable cause for that?
Damn! I'm not sure what we can do.
How about we simply walk up there, knock on the door, and ask them if they are smoking weed?
Well, I guess that would make sense wouldn't it?
Yep.

We got out of the car and walked up the stairs. We knock on the door gently and the door opens. A giant cloud of Marijuana smoke damn near knocks us off the balcony. Doug turns around and looks at me and I just smile. The fool in the doorway wasn't smiling.

"Hey buddy, I'm going to need you to take a few steps back inside for me my friend!"

We stepped inside the apartment and there are two young ladies sitting on the couch, a guy sitting next to one of the girls, and one guy rolled up in a blanket on the floor pretending to be asleep.

The guy that opened the door was the one who lived there and the rest were just visiting to partake in a little herbal action. I asked him where the weed was stashed and he took me to his bedroom and showed me a small amount of marijuana in a baggie that was stashed under his pillow. There was drug paraphernalia all over the apartment and on the dining room table was a huge serving tray that they had turned into their "rolling station". Doug was getting to know the young man that had been pretending to be asleep.

I told the guy on the couch to stand up and patted him down for weapons. Then I told the first young lady, about 21 years old and *very* well put together, to stand up and patted her down for weapons (I have to say, I was a little disappointed not to feel anything that needed to be checked out). Doug finished checking the other girl and I turned to the guy that had opened the door, "*your turn*".

As I was patting him down I noticed a large bulge in the front of his sweatpants, large enough that it looked like it certainly didn't belong there. I said "*what have you got in there*" pointing at his crotch. "Nothing Sir". I said "let's go in the kitchen for a minute". When we got out of sight of the others I told him to turn around and lift his arms. Doug was standing in the dining room area so he could watch the people in the living room and still see us in the kitchen. I reached around and grabbed a handful and started squeezing. I was wearing gloves that I used when I searched people so making out exactly what I was feeling wasn't easy in the first place.

"*What is that hidden in your pants?*" I said, certain that it was a bag of dope.
"*Umm, sir, that's just me*"
That's just you? That's not a bag of dope?
"No sir, that's just my balls and dick"
If that's not a bag of dope I'll salute you!
He pulled the waist of his sweatpants out, I checked……….
And then I saluted him right then and there.

We went back into the living room and I asked the two girls "Which one of you is his girlfriend?" When the girl that I had patted down said that she was, I pointed at her and said "*You are one tough young woman!*" She turned about 6 different shades of red while her friends laughed like crazy.

Since I had molested the young man, and since he had been honest and cooperative, I made him flush the small amount of weed that we had found and gave him, and the others, a warning. "*We know who you are now and we know you like to smoke dope. You all might want to take this opportunity to give it up for good, because I'm going to plaster your pictures, names, addresses, and car descriptions all over the Police Department!*" hoping to discourage them from smoking wacky-weed anymore.

And with that, we left and laughed our asses off the rest of the day.

Working the Hurricanes

One doesn't become a cop to get rich, that's for damn sure. Most cops are so broke they can't pay attention! In order to make ends meet, many law enforcement officers are forced to work off-duty jobs on top of their regular duties. I was certainly no exception to this rule and often worked anywhere from 4 to 14 hours a day at grocery stores, festivals, quinceaneras, concerts, and even disaster areas.

In the early morning hours of August 29, 2005, Hurricane Katrina slammed into the Gulf Coast of Louisiana. The massive storm killed nearly 2000 people and affected more than 90,000 square miles of the United States. Thousands of homes and businesses were destroyed. Looting, rioting, and absolute lawlessness spiraled out of control for weeks.

On September 1, 2008, Hurricane Gustav once again devastated the Louisiana coast, making landfall near Cocodrie, Louisiana. The storm was a powerful one, and 34 parishes were declared disaster areas. One of the small towns hit hardest was Houma, Louisiana.

On September 13, 2008, Hurricane Ike leveled Galveston's outlying communities. Ike made landfall at 2:10 a.m. as a Category 2 hurricane with sustained winds of 110 mph and a 22 foot storm surge. The Bolivar Peninsula was wiped clean. An estimated 100,000 homes were flooded, boats were thrown out of the water ending up on the highway, or in people's yards, and the community's infrastructure was decimated. Galveston was declared uninhabitable and Houston authorities imposed a week-long nighttime curfew.

After each one of these storms I deployed south to work security for a private security firm. While working these jobs, I observed the absolute worst in some people, and the absolute best in others. There are low-life animals on this earth who do not have an ounce of compassion, care for others, or conscience in them and there always will be. I met many of these assholes while I was down there; however, I also met people that gave everything they had to help total strangers. I met people that took displaced strangers into their homes, fed and clothed them, never asking anything in return. Those are the people that keep men and women like me doing what we do.

PEARLAND & BEAUMONT, TEXAS

After Hurricane Katrina, I took time off and went to work in Pearland, Texas just south of Houston for a security firm. My assignment was to watch over a Super Target store. There wasn't much damage in the area, but the electrical grid had been damaged and there was no power in certain parts of the city, this part included.

I drove down in the Ford Explorer that I owned at the time and set up camp in the parking lot. I slept in the SUV for 3 nights, working 12 hour days, before the power had been restored to the store. This was a pretty uneventful job and after the lights came back on I received a call from the security firm, "We need you to head to Beaumont".

As I drove east on Interstate 10 out of Houston, the damage steadily got worse. Signs were down, trees and poles had been laid flat, and the awnings over many gas stations were simply gone. By the time I reached the outskirts of Beaumont, I knew that this job was going to be a lot different than Pearland.

When I reached the city limits of Beaumont, I had to pass through a roadblock that the National Guard had set up. If you were going into the city, you had better have a good reason! I drove up to the guys standing there with their M16's and AR15's. I showed them my credentials and told them that I was headed to a Home Depot store to work security. After inspecting my identification card thoroughly, they allowed me to proceed. They were very professional, but you could tell that they were uneasy.

Getting to the location I was assigned to was not easy. Some of the roads were blocked by downed trees and power poles, and others were flooded. After almost 2 hours, I was able to get to the store. It was 6 miles from the roadblock. When I pulled into the parking lot, it was about 3 a.m. and it was dark. I don't mean it was nighttime, I mean it was pitch black! There were no lights on anywhere that you could see. There was no "light noise" from the city and you couldn't see any stars or the moon, due to the clouds. Every now and then a military truck would drive by on the highway in front of the store, breaking the eerie silence.

It is unbelievable how quiet it can be in the middle of a large city when the entire area has been blacked out. People walking around in the dark looked like zombies from a TV show. The experience reminded me of the movie "Escape from New York". It was hot and the air was sticky due to the high humidity. Mosquitos big enough to wear a saddle were feasting on anybody that was unfortunate enough to be outside.

I climbed in the back of the Explorer to get a couple of hours sleep. It was the first time I had ever slept with my gun right next to me. However, "Slept" may not be the right word to use; it was more like nodding off and waking up every ten minutes. Keep in mind; I was already exhausted from trying to sleep in the car the last three nights. One would think it would be easy to pass out for a few hours, but the entire atmosphere was unlike anything I had ever experienced before. It was truly a disaster zone.

When daylight finally came, the scene around me was surreal. Roofs were torn off buildings, walls had collapsed, giant trees were pushed over, with their roots the size of cars pulled up out of the ground. Debris was everywhere you looked. There was no traffic, a car or military truck here and there, but that was it.

I walked into the store and found my contact, a GI Joe looking man dressed in fatigues. My instructions were simple, "protect the store and its assets using any means necessary". He told me that I would be working the day shift, 6 a.m. to 6 p.m. and another officer would be there at 6 to relieve me for the night. As he was leaving he glanced over his shoulder and said "the Home Depot folks have brought in a bunch of snacks, they are in the break room so make yourself at home and help yourself".

The first week was relatively easy and quiet. The store was closed and there were not many people around that needed to be watched. By that time, I was over sleeping in my car so I was happy when I received a call from the security firm stating that they had found us a hotel room. The only problem; the hotel was over an hour away! I didn't give half a damn, I had not had a shower in over a week, and I desperately needed some sleep.

When 6 o'clock finally arrived, I went to the parking lot and woke up the night shift officer and told him about the hotel room. He was as happy as I was. I threw my stuff in the Explorer and headed west down I-10. About an hour and ten minutes, and 80 miles later, I walked into the greatest hotel room I had ever seen, never mind that it was a rundown Motel 6. I quickly un-assed my clothes and stepped into a hot shower.............Heaven!

I didn't even bother trying to find something to eat, I was too exhausted. I collapsed onto the bed and never moved until my alarm went off at 4:30 the next morning. I remember waking up and not knowing where I was. When the fog finally cleared from my head, it all came back to me and I was relieved. I'm not going to lie; it scared me a little bit. After getting dressed and feeling much better than I had the day before, I grabbed some breakfast at the free buffet on my way out the door and made the trip back to Beaumont.

By this time, the Home Depot people had brought in a giant generator on the back of an 18 wheeler, so the store had power, all be it limited. I had gotten to know the company guys pretty well and asked them if it would be okay for me to use one of the display washing machines on the store floor. They told me to take whatever I needed and have at it.

I took a dolly and moved a nice, (expensive) washing machine out to the garden area. I hooked up a water hose to the machine and then went and found a heavy-duty extension cord and plugged the machine into a wall plug. Next, I went and got a drainage hose and some detergent off the shelf. When I was done, I threw in my, clothing that could almost stand up by itself. After washing my clothes, there was a line of security and other personnel's baskets of clothes lined up on the floor to be washed. I went back to the appliance department and grabbed a dryer with the dolly. I had to move it to the back of the store because that was the only place a 240 plug would work. I didn't even bother running a vent hose to the machine, it just blew out into the building. I was pretty popular that day!

After making the long drive to the hotel and back for about 4 days, a Home Depot Corporate Security Team from California arrived. They had arranged for a travel trailer to be set up at the back of the building for us to sleep in. *NOW WE'RE COOKING WITH CRISCO!*

By this time, Home Depot had brought in additional security personnel to assist us which allowed me to finally take a lunch break during the day. I had been eating snack cakes and granola bars for 8 days and I was going to snap if I didn't get a hot meal. Me and another guy that I had got to know jumped in the car and began driving. After finding nothing open anywhere, I flagged down some National Guard guys and asked them if they knew of anywhere we could get something to eat. They directed us about 12 miles out of town to an intersection where the Red Cross had set up a trailer and was serving Chili Dogs and chips. Let me tell you something, I would have eaten the ass end out of a gassy donkey if they had warmed it up for me! Best chili dogs I've ever had in my life.

During the second week of my stay, the store started bringing in truckloads of generators to sell. The residents of Beaumont still had no power and desperately needed them. The problem: there were hundreds and hundreds of people who wanted to buy a generator, and each truckload could only haul about 24 at a time. Here's where I started earning my money.

We set up a line outside the store with barricades, and started allowing 5 people into the store at a time. One of us was stationed at the entrance and the other at the exit. When 2 or 3 customers would leave, the man at the exit would radio the entrance and tell him to let a couple more in. This worked pretty well for about 4 days, and then the power started coming back on, and guess what happened then? People wanted to return their used, gasoline-filled generators because they didn't need them anymore.

The store had prepared for this to happen; this was not their first rodeo in disaster zones. The store manager declared "The only generators that could be returned for a refund were those that could be proven defective……period!" They brought in people from the generator manufacturer who would inspect each and every returned generator. These guys checked over every single generator to make sure the unit had a legitimate factory defect. If they said yes, then you got a refund. If they said no, then have a nice day and take your new generator back home with you.

Obviously, this didn't go over very well with many people. That's where I came in.

I was cussed out more times than I can count. One lady even threw a shoe at me. One day while this was going on my radio suddenly blew up......"*We need an officer at the front door NOW!*" I took off running and could hear the man before I could even see him. He was yelling as loud as he could and had picked up a shovel and was threatening the manager with it. I drew my gun and walked up behind him to within about 10 feet (I wanted to be as close as possible in case I had to kill this fool so nobody else would be in the line of fire). I ordered him to drop the shovel or I would drop him where he stood. He turned and faced me, ready to bash my head in with that shovel, but when he saw that I meant business, he dropped it. I ordered him to walk outside and told the manager to call 911 to get a Beaumont Officer there in a hurry.

Outside, I holstered my weapon and told him to put his hands behind his back. He told me to fuck off and started walking away. Now, everyone who knows me will tell you that I am a lover, not a fighter. (Stop laughing), but this ole boy was going to jail come hell or high water. I grabbed him and before I could get one of my handcuffs on him, the fight was on!

This big son-of-a-bitch caught me with an elbow right across my chin and it felt like someone had hit me with a bowling ball! When I got over the initial stun of the blow, I went straight for his nuts and landed a punch that had to have flattened his boys! It brought him to his knees and we went at it again. He got to his feet and I grabbed him from behind. He slung me around and we went over the top of a beautiful, $1200 Weber grill, destroying it in an instant. Sometime during this melee, someone standing in line in the front of the store started screaming for help. The front door man had gone to the back of the store to deal with something else just before the fight had started.

The store manager came running out to help me but quickly got punched in the stomach by the big-fisted bastard and he dropped like a sack of hammers. Soon my backup came running out of the store and helped me get Andre the Giant in handcuffs. Now, I'm not going to tell you that I won this fight, because I felt like a bus full of Sumo Wrestlers had run me over, but his big, Cajun, jambalaya-eatin ass went to jail!

I spent 22 days living in that Home Depot store. I met many amazing, good, kind-hearted people and only a handful of total pricks. I spent one night sleeping in a bed at the local hospital sometime during that trip, though I can't really remember exactly when. They had invited us to use any beds that weren't being used for patients. I remember being worried that one of the nurses would think I was a patient and come in to give me an enema or something, but that didn't happen, thank goodness.

Although I don't remember the names of the many guys I worked with during that 3 weeks, this story is dedicated to them for all that they do each day in their own communities.

HOUMA, LOUISIANA

I needed some time away. My second wife and I had separated and were heading toward divorce at break-neck speed. Work was as stressful as ever, and it was time to get my head out of Kaufman for a while. That opportunity presented itself on September 2nd when I heard that the private security firm that I had worked for after Katrina was looking for officers to go to Louisiana, where Hurricane Gustav had left destruction in his path.

I packed my gear and headed southeast. When I arrived at the edge of Terrebonne Parish, late in the evening, the sheriff's department had a roadblock set up on one of the bridges leading into Houma. It was dark so I turned on my interior lights, hoping that my brother coon-asses in uniform could see my "Police" shirt and not open fire on me. They didn't, and after showing them my identification, they told me to be careful and let me pass through.

Getting to my destination, another Home Depot store, in Houma proved to be a challenge. I can't how many times I had to go into the grass to get around something and a few times I had to get out of my truck and physically move tree limbs, trash cans, and even animal carcasses out of the way. I was deep in the heart of alligator country, and I did not like being next to all of the water channels pulling on dead calves and dogs at all!

After a couple hours I made it to the store. Unlike in Beaumont, the store was open, with limited power, but had the same issues with generators. I vividly remembered Andre the Giant and still had a "Weber" impression on my left ass cheek so I was mentally preparing myself for the worst.

The people of south Louisiana were amazing, friendly, and welcoming. I can't begin to tell you all of the food that was brought to the store for us by the people of that community. They are a resilient bunch of folks.

I spent only 8 days in Houma, but its people left a lasting impression on me that I will carry for the rest of my life.

I never did see an Alligator though.

HOUSTON, TEXAS

Three days after returning home from Houma, Louisiana I was called and asked if I wanted to go to Houston because Hurricane Ike was headed straight for Galveston and would hit Houston hard also. I wasn't ready to go back to work, so I extended my vacation and called the security firm back. This time was different, the lady explained to me over the phone. We need you to go to Houston now, ride out the storm in a hotel, and report to your assignment as soon as it's safe to drive.

Say what?

After thinking about it for a minute I decided, what the hell. It will be an experience that I can scratch off my bucket list (not that "*ride out a major hurricane and potentially die*" was on my bucket list). I reloaded my gear, stocked up on food that wouldn't need refrigeration, and headed to Houston. My assignment.....a Home Depot store in a *very* bad part of town, *Yay*!

They sent me to a hotel on the west side of downtown. My room was on the 4th floor and the windows in the room went from the floor to the ceiling, not exactly "hurricane proof". I put my stuff down and went back out to the truck. I wanted to grab a few more things at the grocery store before they closed.

I found a local grocery store and when I walked in I could not believe what I saw. Every shelf was cleaned out! The store looked like it had been looted. The only things left were vegan shit nobody would eat and some damned hummus!

I went and found a hamburger joint that was still open and grabbed a couple of burgers, one for dinner and one for breakfast. I then went back to my hotel room and tried to go to sleep. I knew it would not be getting any rest once old Ike showed up in a couple of hours.

I woke up to the sound of an Amtrak train barreling through my room. I couldn't believe the noise. I got up and went over to the window and pulled the curtains back. *JESUS!!*
I could barely see the lights that were on top of the building directly below my window. I could feel the air pressure in the room increase and decrease. I decided I would lie back down and try to get some more sleep. I noticed that the power was still on. After lying down in my bed, the one closest to the windows, I thought better of it and climbed into the other bed, you know, just in case.

I woke up again sometime later. Something was different. It took me a minute to realize that the power had gone out, but the storm was blowing as much, or more, than it had been earlier. I noticed that I could see some light between the curtains. I pulled them back to reveal that it was now daylight....sort of. It seemed to go dark and then light again within seconds, over and over again.

The trees outside were being blown so hard that they were almost touching the ground. Debris was flying through the air, but something didn't look right. I first thought my glasses were messed up, but then I realized that the damn windows were bowing inward! *Holy Crap!*

I decided I'd better try and grab a shower and get ready to flee this room if those windows gave way. I had thought to bring a small battery operated lantern into the room with me, so I was able to see enough to take a hot shower. Just before I finished, I felt the water turning cold. I must have used the last bit of hot water for the hotel. Well, you snooze, you lose as they say!

I had just finished getting dressed when I received a text that I needed to try and get to my post. *The damn hurricane was still blowing!* But I had told these people I would do the job, and I was going to fulfill that responsibility. I grabbed my bags and headed to the stairwell. As I stepped off of the stairs on the first floor of the hotel, I stepped into 4 inches of water.

I opened the stairwell doors and the first floor was completely flooded. The hallway was full of families with crying kids and people complaining. I was making my way down the hallway when I saw a woman with her 3 kids. She was holding her baby and trying to keep her other two calm. The mother and her two oldest kids were standing in the water, scared to death. I handed her the key card to my room and told her she was welcome to it if she wanted it. I told her there was no power, but at least her kids could get out of the water. She told me thank you and I walked out to my truck. I was soaked to the underwear before I made it inside and shut the door.

There were no traffic lights working. Telephone poles and trees were down everywhere, and power lines stretched across streets. Somehow I made it to Interstate 45. I was the only dumbass on the highway. I remember driving along and I was approaching a bridge underpass. I was in the far right lane when suddenly my truck moved 2 lanes to the left by itself. I never turned the wheel! That is the exact moment when I realized that I am not a very smart man.

Against all odds, I made it to the store on the Far East side of Houston. When I pulled into the parking lot, the "Tuff Sheds" that are set up in every Home Depot parking lot were all over the place, some of them intact, most of them in pieces. Several had been blown up against a fence on the north side of the property. I had to pee so bad I was seeing fish swimming around in front of my eyeballs.

I pulled over to the pile of buildings and got out of my truck. I made my way around behind a couple of the buildings that were partially intact and let it fly. I was enjoying this sweet relief when I heard a truck pull into the parking lot. I finished and zipped up, and then I eased over to where I could see the vehicle but still stay hidden. A dark green colored 4-door Ford pickup slowly drove up close to the building and then drove over to within 50 yards of my truck. I could see two Hispanic men in the front seat and they were talking and pointing to my truck as they looked all around.

"These sorry bastards are going to try and steal my truck!"

The thought of these vultures trying to steal a truck, *my truck*, during a freakin hurricane pissed me off and pissed me off good! I decided to wait until they made their move. They weren't too sure about the truck and why nobody was around it. They made another slow circle of the parking lot, but I knew they weren't leaving. Scum like these never leave an easy target.

Just like I figured it, they made their way back down to my truck, but this time they pulled up about 20 feet behind it. A Hispanic man climbed out of the backseat. *"Damn, I don't know how many are in there!"* But at that moment, it didn't really matter. I was mad. There were at least three of them and I had eight bullets in the gun in my hand. *"Bring your sorry asses on"* I said out loud to myself.

I waited until the thieving piece of shit made it to the tailgate of my truck and then I came out screaming at the top of my lungs that I was going to blow his mother-fucking head off! He was so scared he busted his ass trying to run back to the truck. I pointed my gun at the face of the driver as he threw the truck into reverse and squalled the tires. He damned near ran over his accomplice before he was able to make it back in the truck. I never saw those truck stealing assholes again.

I climbed into my truck and pulled over to the awning where they load lumber at, backed in, and waited for the adrenaline dump crash, while I ate some Captain Crunch cereal out of the box. I thought to myself, *Ain't that a bitch!*

The job was pretty much the same as the other times I had worked at Home Depot. I had to sleep in my truck, but it was pretty easy to pass out knowing that I had other guys watching out for me while I snoozed. They had brought in the same snacks as each time before.....crackers, cookies, chips, granola bars, pop-tarts, etc. and like before, I was sick of all the junk after two days. They finally did bring in pizza one day and we had hopes of at least eating hot pizza for a while, but the pizza restaurant had to close shortly after that due to no electricity or water.

After about 11 days, I decided that I was going to get a hot meal if I had to drive back to Dallas to get it. I drove around the depressed neighborhood and spotted a small taco stand that had a line with about 20 people in it. *Meet number 21 baby!* I had to wait over an hour, but those were the best damn tacos I ever had and I didn't give a damn if they were beef, chicken, chorizo, or kangaroo, they were great!

I bout about 15 of those tacos and took them back to the store. I stashed a couple in my truck and took the rest in to the other security guys and the store manager. One giant black man named "Tank" told me he was going to make love to me after he finished his tacos……thank the good lord he was joking because he was so huge and strong that I would have just had to bend over and asked him to be gentle.

I had a few skirmishes down there but nothing major. I was offered a job anytime I ever needed one by the store manager before I left. He was a good guy and I had saved his butt a few times from angry customers. Angry asses are my specialty!

I spent 17 days at that store in Houston, and like the other times, I met some awesome people. I am truly thankful to the lord above that I am in a place today where I don't have to work like that anymore. I'm too out of shape and too old to be standing on my feet for 14 hours a day. I will always be thankful for the memories that the lord gave me during those trips. I was able to help out a lot of people, made a lot of money, and came out of it all relatively unscathed.

To this day, I have a fear of Weber grills though.

The Kaufman County DA Murders............
My Perspective.

Thursday January 31, 2013.........8:43 a.m. a masked gunman dressed in all black walks up to Kaufman County Assistant District Attorney Mark Hasse as he was walking from his truck to the courthouse to report for work. According to a witness, the coward hiding behind the mask said something to Mark and he responded by pleading "I'm sorry" but his words were interrupted as bullets were fired into his body. According to the witness, the assassin then fired several shots in the air from a second gun before running to his getaway car and fleeing the area. Mark never had a chance to pull the gun he had in his briefcase.

For the last month, I had been attending the Institute for Law Enforcement Administration's "School of Police Supervision" program in Arlington, Texas. On the morning of January 31st I was in Plano, Texas at the Institutes' headquarters with my beautiful wife Leslie, and my amazing daughter Chelsea, my first born. I was graduating from the program and was full of pride for having completing the program, even though no one from the Police Department saw fit to be there. It was typical behavior of the department's management at the time. If it didn't affect them directly, they didn't give a shit.

I had just walked across the stage and received my program diploma when my phone started going crazy. The messages I kept receiving read *"Call the department immediately 911!"* I stepped out into the foyer and called the office. The call set in motion four months of long, hard hours of work, mixed emotions, and career impacting decisions. It went like this:

"This is Black, what's going on?"
"Captain, Mark Hasse has been shot and killed on the courthouse square. The killer took off and is at-large"
"Do we know who the suspect is?"
"No sir"
"What's going on at the scene?"
"All of our people are out there, KSO has all of their people out there, and we are waiting on the DPS Crime Scene unit to arrive, The Texas Rangers are also in route"
"Where is Doug?"

"He is at the scene"
"Okay, tell him to call me immediately"
"Yes sir"

I hung up and went inside to tell Leslie and Chelsea that I had to leave. We were all disappointed. I had planned to take them to a nice lunch to celebrate, but there was nothing I could do about it and they understood that.
Sergeant Doug Barker, one of our Criminal Investigators, and my good friend, called me. He told me that DPS was going to work the crime scene and that he was on his way to the Southwest Institute of Forensic Sciences (SWIFS) in Dallas to attend Mark's autopsy.

I then called the Chief of Police and he asked me to head to Dallas and assist Doug at the autopsy. I then kissed Chelsea goodbye, and told Leslie to take me to SWIFS near downtown Dallas. I don't remember the drive to the Medical Examiner's office, although I'm sure I pretty much ignored Leslie the entire way there with a million things going through my mind at the speed of light. I had just talked to Mark Hasse four days earlier, and Doug had been in his office two days before. "*What the hell?*"

Doug and I arrived at SWIF's at about the same time. I kissed Leslie, told her to drive safe and I would see her whenever I was able to go home. Who knew when that would be? I met up with Doug and we went inside. Two Investigators from the Kaufman County Sheriff's Department also arrived to attend the examination of Mark's body. I was glad to see them; I knew we would need a lot of help on this one. Little did I, or anyone else, know that this case was about to become a dark part of American history.

Most people have no idea what it's like to attend an autopsy. It is not an experience for the faint of heart. You walk in to what amounts to a very large operating room, about half the size of a basketball court. The first thing you do is put disposable shoe covers over your shoes, and then you stand out of the way until the doctor calls you over. If you get there early in the morning, you get to watch them roll in all of the bodies that had been delivered the day and night before.

Autopsies

Each body is rolled over to one of many identical examination stations and then removed from the body bag and placed onto a stainless steel table. The doctor assigned to each body then performs the exact same procedures, every time, from start to finish. I am certainly not a doctor, but the following is what I remember from the numerous autopsies that I have attended over the years:

First the body is lined up on the examination table with the head propped onto a cradle-like object to keep it from moving.
Next, the examiner photographs the body from every angle, including bringing over a ladder and climbing up above the body for photos from that position.
Then the body is meticulously examined and any item, no matter how small or insignificant one might think it is, such as a leaf or grass, is collected and placed into evidence containers.
The body is then washed.
When the doctor is ready to start the autopsy, they slice straight down the front of the body from the center of the chest to below the belly button. The doctor then slices from the center of the chest out to each shoulder. Picture a "T" placed over the front of a body. He or she then cuts out from the bottom of the center cut and folds the skin back on each side of the body revealing the ribs and intestines.
The examiner then grabs a set of tree pruners, yes I said tree pruners, just like you buy at the hardware store, and chops each rib on each side of the rib cage until the entire rib cage can be lifted out of the body, revealing all of the internal organs.
Each organ is then removed one at a time, placed in a scale that looks exactly like the scales you see in a grocery store produce section, and weighed. After the weight is recorded, a small sample may be taken from the organ for analysis. It is then placed into a red colored "Hazmat" bag.
Once all of the organs are removed and placed into the bag, it's time to get the brain out.
For this task, the doctor utilizes a "Dremel" type tool with a cutting disk, just like people cut metal with.

The skull is cut all the way around the head, just above the eyebrows. They then take a chisel and hammer and pry the skull apart until it breaks free.
Next, the brain is cut away from the brain stem, taken out of the skull, and is also weighed and examined.
When the examining doctor is finished, they place the big, red "Bag-O-Guts" down into the body cavity, and a tech comes and gets the body to be prepared for release to a funeral home.

Sometimes when I have attended autopsies, there have been 10-12 bodies around the room. All naked, some with visible stab or bullet wounds, some with severe burns, and some with an aroma that can peel paint off a wall (Kelley Osgan's body had seemed to bring even the most seasoned examiner to their knees) The only time I ever had any issues was when there was a child's body in the room, in those cases, I never looked in that direction. I couldn't handle those. I was blessed by never having to attend a child's autopsy.

Mark's body was lying there and we could see the entry wounds the bullets had made as they tore through him. We were patiently waiting behind the designated red line painted on the floor, trying not to look at him as the man we knew, but simply as evidence. We mostly failed in our endeavors to do that.

Doug had only attended one or two of the procedures before this, so he hadn't quite learned all of the rules yet. So when the doctor came over and began his examination, Doug was paying very close attention to every word he was saying, which was fine. The problem came when the doctor saw him writing down what he was saying. That is a big no-no!

"If you write down anything I am saying I will have your ass thrown out of here!"

He was not playing. Doug was startled and instantly threw his notepad on the nearby table as only he could do………."*I ain't heard shit Doc!*" He said, as I tried not to bust out laughing. As I have stated earlier in this book, Doug Barker was just naturally the funniest human being I have ever met.

After the autopsy was completed, we headed back to Kaufman and went directly to the crime scene. The Kaufman County Sheriff's Department had set up their Mobile Command Post trailer and the Texas Department of Public Safety had brought along theirs as well. I watched as numerous officers photographed, measured, and searched the entire area. I could still see the dark colored blood on the ground where Mark had fallen.

The scene at the time of the shooting, and in the hours following, was absolute organized chaos. Witnesses were each describing the gunman's getaway vehicle as a different make, model, and color. *It was a brown Ford. It was a maroon car. It was a tan sedan, etc.* Nobody knew who, or what, they were looking for, which is often the case in a situation like that. One of the key witnesses, a local attorney who was pulling up as the shooter was fleeing, couldn't even tell us what kind of car it was. It soon became clear that the scum that had killed Mark Hasse, for now anyway, had escaped capture.

Later that day, officers were spread out in the city looking for anybody that may have seen or heard something, *anything!* Investigators were sent out to collect every second of surveillance video that might be available from homes and businesses around the area. By that evening every square inch of the neighborhood just north of the crime scene had been searched on foot; one of the very few things that we were certain of in those hours immediately following the murder was that the suspect had come from, and fled to, the north of the scene.

The Incident Command Post

The next morning, the National Guard Armory was converted into an Incident Command Post (ICP). I was "appointed" as the "Commander" of the ICP by the man who was then the Chief of Police. He had retired from the Dallas Police Department and had absolutely no clue how a small agency operated. His appointment baffled me. He informed me that we were going to run this investigation, not anyone else.

There were dozens of men and women that were working on the case, from the FBI to the Texas Rangers, to the Sheriff of

Kaufman County, that had many more years of experience than I did in working homicides, but this guy wanted me telling them what to do. *No thank you!* My intent was to help them in any way I could, stay out of their way, and learn as much as possible, and that is exactly what I did.

The National Guard Armory building looked like most posts do; it was a large, open building with a roll-up bay door at the far end. As you walk into the building, there are restrooms and a kitchen on the left side. On the right side were classrooms and on the front wall were a couple of small offices.

As the ICP got up and running, we were working 14-16 hour days. We would go home just long enough to get a shower and a few hours rest and then head straight back in and pick up where we left off. The FBI had sent in their "Critical Incident Response Group" (CIRG) out of Dallas, and this group of people was impressive.

They came in to a bare, empty building and, literally overnight, had a fully operational Command Center, complete with computers, printers, scanners, and large computer monitors that displayed all of the information for the tips that had been received, vetted, and followed up on, along with the tips that were waiting to be investigated. They had set up separate work stations for each process that had to be completed in order to keep track of each and every tip that was phoned in, every person that had been talked to, and the actions of each officer.

The building, at that time, had no working telephones, other than the one in the front office. In 12 hours the CIRG Team had dozens of phone lines up and operational. They established a telephone tip line and had personnel manning the phones day and night. Their team set up a computer program to track each tip, who it was assigned to, what had been done to follow up on that tip, and the result of the follow up; without this program, it would have been impossible to keep up with all of the data from the thousands of tip-line calls.

With the non-stop chaos going on and law enforcement personnel numbers that surpassed 100 working on the case, you can imagine how hard it would be to get everyone some time for lunches and breaks, however, we never even had a chance to worry about that issue thanks to the people of Kaufman, Texas.

The Kaufman community took it upon themselves to feed all of us; and man did they ever feed us! I have never seen more food delivered to a single place, hour after hour and day after day, than I did the entire time we were there. It was amazing! People would cook homemade meals and bring them to us. Businesses were bringing in drinks by the pallet-load. Civic groups and clubs were collecting everything from snacks to headache medicine, from cell phone chargers to pens and notebooks.

But the absolute favorite items for everyone were the thank you cards, posters, and letters that the school children were constantly making for us. When we would start to get tired or frustrated, one look at those messages from the kids was like a shot of adrenaline to our systems. And it certainly didn't stop there; everywhere I went people would shake my hand and offer any assistance they could, some people would hug me, some would pray for me. It was an experience that instilled in me the knowledge that most of the community really does care about us.

Inside the Incident Command Post, once you stepped away from the food and gifts from our citizens, there were many different dynamics, and power struggles constantly at work. It was an extremely tense and stressful atmosphere. Anytime you have multiple law enforcement entities working on the same case, in the same building, for days and weeks at a time, you are going to have conflict, but this was something altogether different than anything I had ever experienced before. I can't count the number of times I said to myself "*I thought we were all on the same team?*"

Every single member of the Kaufman Police Department's Command Staff, except the new Chief that had been there less than 6 months, wanted to hand the case off to the larger agencies, who had far more experience, equipment, and funding, and continue to help in a support capacity. But the Chief was not having any of it. This was his time in the spotlight, and he intended to milk every minute of it that he possibly could.

He set himself up in one of the offices at the front of the building, stuck his name on the door and claimed his fiefdom. He was constantly calling meetings and dragging people away from their assignments to go over the same information time and time again. After a few days of this, we started hearing people talking shit and laughing at him, which we tolerated because we were basically doing the same thing. Soon after though, the ridicule started trickling down to the entire Kaufman Police Department. This disrespect, however, would not be tolerated, and it created a lot of division and hard feelings between the officers, deputies, and agents.

One day I came out of the "Strategy Room" and overheard a group of people from several different agencies talking about the "Riot Jacket Twins". I noticed that when one member of the group saw me, he tapped the woman next to him and suddenly everyone got quiet. I knew, and had worked alongside, one of the Deputies that were standing there, so a few minutes later I caught him in the kitchen area and asked him what the hell that was all about. He could tell that I was irritated I guess, so he told me to follow him outside. I did so and he filled me in on the covert conversation.

Apparently, there were two members of our department that had set themselves up, or had been set up, at a table toward the back of the building. I was told this is where they stayed anytime they were in the building. They were both always wearing black and white "POLICE" jackets and had been dubbed the "Raid Jacket Twins" by someone at the sheriff's department. Their running joke was that it was the job of the "Riot Jacket Twins" to keep the table from escaping, because they were never seen doing anything else. I was pissed off, and I told him so, but I had more important things going on than to worry about blowing that up at the time.

To say that I had been embarrassed by the Chief of Police and his behavior would be a huge understatement. I was embarrassed by a couple of other members of my department as well, but nothing compared to what the Chief had caused. One morning I was speaking to a high-ranking member of local law enforcement and we were discussing the amazingly large amount of "Idiot" that can fit inside one human being. He quietly told me to follow him and he led me to the 'Throne Room", which is what they had named the Chief's office. He opened the door and I followed him inside and watched as he grabbed a book off of the table that the King had been using as his desk. He handed me the book and I could not believe my eyes. The title of the book was "Homicide Investigation: An Introduction" written by John J. Miletich. This was the Chief of Police that represented me and my department. The only way it could have been worse is if the book had been titled "Homicide for Dummies!"

I began distancing myself from the "leader" of my own department. At one point, his behavior became so bad that a Captain of the Texas Rangers arrived at the Command Post from Austin and pulled the man into his own office. I was not there, but the meeting was apparently pretty intense because everyone was talking about it when I returned.

The final straw came when it was learned that he had (allegedly) withheld information that was crucial to the investigation. At that point, he was kicked out of the Command Center and told not to return by the Texas Rangers. *The Chief of Police was kicked out of the Command Center people!* From that point forward, the officers of the Kaufman Police Department, who had been killing themselves on this case, were ostracized and shunned. We were left out of crucial intelligence meetings and briefings. This was an absolute low point in my career for me. I was being looked at by the other agencies as if they couldn't trust me, and that bullshit was completely unacceptable. I left the Command Center and did not go back.

One Last Kick in the Nuts

My relationship with the Chief of Police rapidly deteriorated to one of absolute disgust. I avoided him at all costs, and when we did speak, it was never pleasant. At one point, I told him to go to hell and walked out of his office. This is not behavior that I am proud of, but by then, he was an embarrassment to me, my officers, and my profession. *I simply did not give a damn about rank at this point.*

Soon after this investigation was completed, the Chief announced his resignation. He had been hired by another agency in the DFW Metroplex. This announcement was music to my ears however there would be one last kick in the nuts for me where he was concerned.

The week before the Chief was to leave I overheard a conversation outside my office that forever changed my outlook on police work. That was the day I decided that I didn't want to do this work anymore. I didn't want to be associated with certain people anymore. I had a huge decision to make.

The Chief of Police and the City Manager at that time had secretly appointed a Sergeant to be the Interim Chief. *A fucking Sergeant, over me, a Captain* This Sergeant was the one that I had beaten out for the job of Captain. He had been hired in at the rank of Sergeant about a year before this and was a retired Dallas cop. You see, I had one huge flaw that I simply couldn't overcome; I had never worked for the Dallas Police Department.

That was the nail in my coffin where the City Manager was concerned. He had hired the previous Chief from Dallas PD, then he hired the current Chief from Dallas, and now he had another DPD retiree waiting in the wings. That day I learned that years of dedication and service to this department meant absolutely nothing. It was the first time in my career I had really allowed myself to believe that. There were times when I thought it was true, a lot of past officers of the department had said as much, but I had never accepted it as fact until that day. I never felt the same dedication to the city after that day.

When word got around that I was thinking about leaving Kaufman, I was contacted and offered a job by 2 different agencies in the area, but after taking a couple of weeks to think about it and talk to my family, I decided to go ahead and finish my career in Kaufman. I loved the community, the people, and the small town aspect of the job. However, no matter how hard I tried, my heart and soul was no longer in the work. For the first time ever, it was just a job.

The Nightmare Continues

On March 30, 2013 at about 7:00 p.m. I was at home relaxing, standing at my barbecue grill, cooking some filets and enjoying a cold beer when my phone rang. The number showed it to be the other Captain of the department. I answered and his words hit me like a fist to the stomach. The Kaufman County District

Attorney Mike McLelland, and his wife Cynthia, had been found murdered inside their home in Forney. They weren't just killed, they had been slaughtered.

Someone out there was stalking and assassinating members of our District Attorney's Office; a place where friends of mine worked, people that I talked to on a regular basis. This didn't happen in Kaufman County. We were a small, rural community where tractors still held up traffic on the main roads. This was something else, something straight out of Hollywood.

I hung up the phone and immediately called my good friends Dian and Ricky Floyd's son Daniel, who was a prosecutor in the District Attorney's office. When he answered the phone I could tell that he had been upset and was scared. His voice was cracking as we spoke;

"Daniel, this is Ed. Where are you?"
"I'm at home, what the hell is going on Eddie?"
"I don't know bud, but I need you and Lori to stay at your house with the doors locked and do not open it for anyone that you don't know okay?"
"Okay, we will"
"If I hear of anything that you need to know I will call you at this number"
"Thanks man"
"No problem, just do what I say"

I made several other phone calls and learned that the wheels had been put in motion to get security for each member of the DA's office until we could get a handle on what was happening.
I called my friend Dian to let her know that I would personally go sit outside her son and daughter-in-law's home to protect them if it came to that. She knew I meant what I said.

Over the course of the next few days the courthouse square in Kaufman was a 3-ring media circus. Satellite trucks from all over the country were arriving by the hour. Reporters were talking to anyone and everyone that they could get to stand still for a few seconds. Everywhere I went I was approached by reporters wanting me to say something, anything, that they could take and run with. I tried to explain to them that our department was not the lead agency on the McClelland case but they didn't care. I'm sure they were doing it to every other officer in the city as well. Our officers were under strict orders not to speak to anyone about the case. I was proud that they all followed those orders without exception.

On top of the reporters, I had citizens coming up to me every time I left the office. Some of them were just curious and were hoping for some gossip, but most of them just wanted some assurance that our small community was safe for them and their families. My heart went out to those people. I could see the fear in their eyes. My comments were almost always the same *"We have the best that Texas law enforcement and the FBI has to offer here working on this thing. Kaufman is the safest place in the state right now"*.

The Prime Suspect

If you followed the investigation through the media, then you know that many different theories came up as the days and weeks passed. The Aryan Brotherhood, prison gangs, an escaped inmate from Colorado; hell I think Kim Jong Un was even rumored at one point or another of playing a part in all three murders. For the investigators of the Kaufman Police Department, and for many members of the Kaufman County Sheriff's Department, there was never any question; it was Eric Williams that did it. *We just had to prove it!*

Eric Lyle Williams is a demented, arrogant, and pure evil serial killer. He was also just plain weird. One of our officers once rolled up on him at 2:00 a.m. riding his "Segway" in his pajama shorts, with an AR-15 slung across his back by a sling. He said he was "patrolling the neighborhood". I mean really, this was one thrown-off piece of shit.

Several years before the murders, Williams had been accused of over-billing the county for work he allegedly performed as a court-appointed attorney for CPS (Child Protective Services) cases. When he was questioned about his bills, he got pissed off and removed himself from the list of attorneys that would perform the work. Unfortunately for him, he had one little problem. The CPS casework was where he made almost all of his money, so after he got over his mad spell, he promptly signed back up. I was told that they kept a very close eye on his billing habits after that.

Williams had been elected as the Precinct 1 Justice of the Peace, and took office in January of 2011. Just five months later, in May of 2011, he was captured on video stealing computers from the county's Information and Technology Department. On April 10, 2012 he was sentenced to 2 years of probation and had to surrender his law license. Mark Hasse and Mike McLelland had aggressively prosecuted Williams. Mike believed that a public servant who would steal from the very people he was elected to serve was the lowest of the low.

It was learned that Williams was a member of the Texas National Guard, (Coincidentally, so was the Kaufman Chief of Police) and had been a law enforcement officer in the past. He owned enough guns to stock a firearms store. He had many different weapons and he knew how to use them. This is not a good combination when you are talking about an egocentric, delusional psychopath.

I used to see him 2 or 3 times a week out having lunch at local restaurants. It's a small town and there weren't a lot of choices for restaurants, so it was quite common to run into the same people during the week at different dining establishments. Most of the time when I would see him, he was with Judge Glen Ashworth (Retired).

Judge Ashworth, it is my understanding, had helped him get his start in the field of law and I had always assumed that they were good friends. You can imagine my surprise when I learned that Williams had placed the judge at the top of his hit list as one of his next victims. Judge Ashworth's residence backed up to the rear of Williams's in-law's house. From there, the coward assassin planned to shoot the judge with a crossbow when he found the judge in his backyard.

But just shooting the man with a piercing arrow wasn't good enough for this nut job, he had planned to cut open Ashworth's belly, pour in some homemade Napalm, and then set him on fire. *That is some serious anger right there!* (And just as a side note, they did find several jars of homemade Napalm in Williams' storage building.)

Eric Williams and his wife Kim lived about 200 feet from the edge of the Incident Command Post property. He had a perfect view of all the activity outside the command post day and night. He would drive by every day, no doubt laughing his ass off at the small army of cops that were trying to figure out that he was the one that committed the killings. He had a front row seat to the entire investigation and he loved it.

He had been interviewed soon after the murder of Mark Hasse and had consented to a Gunshot Residue Test (GSR). Hell, why not, he had been wearing gloves! The FBI had interviewed him and decided he was not the killer, so they pushed the investigation in another direction. Mike McLelland and many others, however, were very vocal and adamant throughout the investigation...*ERIC WILLIAMS DID IT!* Unfortunately, the pieces just never fell into place to prove it until it was too late.

Eric's happy, homicidal life came crashing down when a buddy of his in the Texas National Guard contacted authorities and let them in on a little secret.....he had rented a storage unit in Seagoville, Texas in his name, for Eric. The storage unit turned out to be the mother-lode.

The Kaufman Police Department was left completely in the dark when all of this information came to light. We weren't even notified when they served the search warrant on the storage building, despite the fact that we were still, technically, the lead agency in the Hasse murder investigation. This was the ultimate slap in the face from one agency to another. But the absolute worst part for me was the knife that they shoved in the back of Doug Barker, our Lead Investigator on the Hasse case.

Doug had worked for weeks side by side at the Command Post with deputies and agents that he considered close friends. He worked his ass off for those people and was purposely left out of the loop when the biggest break of the cases started coming together, for something that he had absolutely nothing to do with. It wasn't his fault that the Chief couldn't be trusted. Among law enforcement officers, this kind of thing is the ultimate act of betrayal and as far as I am concerned, those that were a part of the decision to do that to him are cowards.

Some of those people I had worked with for more than 10 years. Many friendships and professional relationships were permanently damaged because of this disrespectful, selfish, and unnecessary decision. To this day, there are investigators at our neighboring agency that I will not work with. *I mean really, if you couldn't trust me then, why the hell would you trust me now?* And what was really the icing on the cake, is that they played it off like they "forgot" to let us know. They didn't even have the guts to stand up and tell us the truth until much later.

The Conviction

Eric Williams was convicted of Capital Murder in the death of Cynthia McLelland on December 4, 2014 in Rockwall, Texas. The trial had been moved when the defense filed for a change of venue. He was not tried for the murders of Mark Hasse or Mike McLelland, (a legal strategy). On December 17th, as he sat looking smug in the courtroom, the jury handed down the death penalty for his gutless and cowardly acts. His wife, Kim Lene Williams, had previously pled guilty in exchange for her testimony against her husband and given a 40 year prison sentence. She is currently serving her time at the Murray Unit in Gatesville, Texas and is eligible for parole in April of 2033.

Williams continues to file appeals, claiming everything from "the judge was mean to me", to his brain is "broken" (Well no shit Sherlock, nobody with a normal brain becomes a serial killer!). Hopefully, I will live to see the day they send him to hell.

Afterthoughts

Mark, Mike, and Cynthia had all dedicated their lives to helping people. It is something that was inside them, not something they woke up one day and decided to do. It is the same thing that is inside every good law enforcement officer. It is what calls you to keep going back day after day, week after week, and year after year.

A weak and worthless person took them from their families and friends, hiding behind a mask and uniform like all cowards do. But he was unable to accomplish the one thing he wanted most;

the only thing that could give him the satisfaction that his warped mind had to have....he was unable to erase these great people from the hearts and minds of everyone that knew them. He failed miserably at that.

I had the pleasure of working with Mark Hasse and Mike McLelland. I never had the opportunity to meet Cynthia, although I have heard nothing but good things about the woman who loved to quilt and bake treats for those around her.

I can say this without hesitation; the world needs more people like them in it.

Cross erected at the site where Kaufman County Assistant District Attorney Mark Hasse was gunned down. Photo by Edward Black

This Story is Dedicated to the Memory of Mark Hasse and Mike & Cynthia McLelland.

Do nothing out of selfish ambition or vain conceit. Rather, in humility value others above yourselves,

Philippians 2:3

Aubrey Wright Hawkins 1971-2000

Officer Aubrey Hawkins at KPD

When I started as a Reserve Police Officer at the Kaufman Police Department in 1996, Aubrey was one of the officers who helped trained me. He was a great officer and trainer, as well as just a great man. He was always smiling, but when it came time to do the job, he was all business.

One of my favorite memories of Aubrey is when I was out patrolling on my own shortly after being released from the FTO program and I made a traffic stop. The man I stopped did not speak English at all, so I called Aubrey over and asked for his assistance. Aubrey was able to speak and understand Spanish, although my memory fails me if he was fluent or just spoke enough to get by on the streets.

Aubrey arrived and I told him what I need help with. We walked up to the truck and handled the stop without incident. The traffic stop lasted about 10 minutes and Aubrey went on like everything was just hunky-dory. As we completed the interaction with the driver and were walking back to our patrol cars, Aubrey put his arm around me, smiled, and said *"Hey bud, you might want to go to the station and grab your gun"*. He then went on to his car like nothing had even been said. I looked down and my holster was as empty as it could be!

Just before the traffic stop I had made an arrest and booked the man into our jail. When you book a prisoner into jail you are required to secure your weapon in a locked cabinet. Me, being a relatively new young officer, had completely forgot to retrieve my gun when I left the station!

I drove back to the station as fast as I could and grabbed my weapon. I felt like a complete dummy. A few minutes later, Aubrey came in and I guess he could tell that I was embarrassed about it, so he came over to me and told me that he had done the same thing two times before himself. I don't know if he really had or not, but he made me feel better about the whole thing. That was just the kind of man he was.

From the Irving Police Department website...

On December 24, 2000, at 6:29 p.m., Officer Aubrey Hawkins was dispatched to a suspicious circumstance call at the Oshman's Sporting Goods Store at State Highway 183 and Belt Line Road. Officer Hawkins took the call from a restaurant less than one mile away where he had just finished eating Christmas Eve dinner with his wife, Lori, his son, his mother, and grandmother.

Aubrey arrived before any other units and approached from the north entrance, using the service road. He drove through the parking lot looking at the front of the business then around the south side to the rear of the building. As he made it to the west side loading dock area and entered the driveway, he came under a barrage of gunfire without warning and had no time to take evasive or defensive action. Mortally wounded, Officer Hawkins was pulled from his squad car and run over by the killers.

What had begun as a suspicious circumstance call turned out to be a robbery-in-progress committed by seven dangerous and violent escaped prisoners (known as the Texas 7) from the Texas Department of Corrections Facility in Huntsville, Texas, earlier that month. It was later learned that a lookout to the east of the store had seen his approach and warned the others causing them to abandon the numerous store employees that were huddled together, and bound, inside the store. Officer Hawkins' arrival to the dock area had coincided with the exit, from the building, of the escaped convicts providing them with an overwhelming advantage. Following the murder of Officer Hawkins, international media coverage followed the largest manhunt in Texas history. The manhunt ended in January 2001 in the communities of Woodland Park and Colorado Springs, Colorado, with the suicide of one escapee and the nonviolent capture of the other six after law enforcement located and descended upon them.

Five of the cowards have been sent to hell already and the other two are still rotting away on Death Row at the Polunsky Unit in Livingston, Texas. I, along with several other officers in the department, travelled to Huntsville for the execution of George Rivas, the group's leader and the mastermind of their escape, on February 29, 2012.

Blessed are the peacemakers: for they shall be called the children of God.
Matthew 5:9

The Status of the Texas 7- December 2017

- Donald Keith Newbury *executed.*
- George Angel Rivas, Jr. *executed.*
- Michael Anthony Rodriguez *executed.*
- Joseph Christopher Garcia *executed.*
- Larry James Harper committed suicide before he could be captured by law enforcement.
- Randy Ethan Halprin on Texas Death Row awaiting execution.
- Patrick Henry Murphy, Jr. on Texas Death Row awaiting execution.

The Captain's Take on the State of Law Enforcement In 2017

I have been on the "inside" of law enforcement looking out for the last 20 years and that, along with the fact that I subscribe to the belief that justice should apply equally to every citizen, I feel gives me a unique perspective on the state of affairs in this country where the enforcement of law is concerned.

I believe that every person, every single person, is entitled to the protection of the law to the exact same degree as every other person. Unfortunately, that is not what's happening in the United States of America today. The system is broken and will probably never be fixed.

The Criminal Justice System's foundation is the Constitution of the United States, but it's very base is our law enforcement Officer. Everything relating to the justice system begins with the cop who is out there taking reports, patrolling neighborhoods, and arresting criminals. He is who you call when your daughter's bicycle is stolen, or your garage is broken into. He is who you call when your husband is beating the hell out of you again. He is the one you call when your child has left a suicide note and can't be found, or when your elderly father has unexplained bruises all over him at the nursing home. Everything begins with the law enforcement officer. So why are the leaders of this country doing everything in their power to keep him from being able to do his job?

The answer is pretty simple……..*greed*.

Let me explain; lawmakers make a lot of money. Lawmakers are elected officials. Elected officials want to continue being elected officials. In order to do that, they need people to vote for them. To get people to vote for them, they pick certain topics that their class of voters are pissed off about, and they vote whichever way makes them look good with said voters. The current generation hates cops. The current generation also votes. Therefore, the rich, elected lawmakers vote for whatever is going against the cops the most; hence they are re-elected and keep making a lot of money. This repeats every year and the cycle never stops.

Some of you are laughing your ass off right now but think about it for a minute before dismissing me totally. At this point in time we are living in an "anti-law enforcement" country. We hold the cops responsible for every bad thing that happens and we completely exonerate the criminal from any wrong doing. The exact wrong doing that led to the bad thing happening in the first place!

In every officer-involved shooting, especially if the bad guy is a different race from the officer that shot him, the first thing that happens is the cop is put on trial in the media. Not the individual that had been robbing, stealing from, and assaulting people his entire life, no, the man who has dedicated his life to helping others is publicly tried and convicted before any kind of investigation can be completed.

There are three things that happen after every police involved shooting now. The first thing that happens is that the greedy, ambulance chasing scum that we call defense attorneys, get a group of church ladies together and hold a press conference on the front steps of the Police Department or City Hall, and demand that the officer involved be immediately terminated and prosecuted.

The second thing that happens is the Police Chief comes out and tries to explain that an investigation is under way and nothing will be decided before the conclusion of the investigation because that's the right thing to do.

The third thing that happens is the self-appointed "activists" publicly attack the Chief of Police and threaten to go after the City Manager or Mayor next. An emergency meeting is then called and the Chief of Police is ordered to terminate the involved officer immediately, or *his* ass is out. Ladies and gentlemen, welcome to the justice system for police 2017 edition.

Let's get something straight here; I am not talking about out and out bad shootings okay. Some of these incidents are absolutely black and white. The situations where a cop simply murders someone are off the table, and there have been a few of them in recent times. The killing of Walter Scott in South Carolina and Laquan McDonald in Chicago are just a couple. Those officers killed men when they did not have to and should be, and have been, punished just like anyone else. There is no justification for shooting any person who is not an immediate danger to the officer or another human being.

We now live in a society that accepts, and excuses, criminal behavior. People do not demand dignified and respectful behavior from others because they are now being raised to believe that it is perfectly acceptable to steal if someone has something that you want. The kids are taught that if someone "disrespects" you, then you must hurt them or you are weak. The citizens of our "hug-a-thug" country now make excuses for the criminals, instead of holding them accountable for their actions.

How many times have you watched a news story about a punk that was breaking into someone's home, who was shot and killed by the homeowner, and the criminal's family is on television yelling about how good a person he was?

Oh really?

It's funny that their families never get around to telling the reporters about his 14 arrests, his drug habit, or the 6 kids he has by 6 different women, none of whom he pays a single penny of child support to.

I am not generalizing or profiling any one group, they come in all races, genders, and religions. My point is the criminal is excused for their behavior, no matter what they did or how many people they hurt. Especially, if they hurt or kill a Police Officer. This has got to stop people. We, as Americans, deserve better than this!

We, as a country, must start sending the message, loud and clear, that we will not tolerate these thugs, punks, and cowards continuing to assault our Law Enforcement Officers. We must also send the message that if you do attack a Peace Officer, then you will automatically pay a very heavy price.

A conviction for intentionally murdering a Law Enforcement Officer should be an automatic death sentence. If you intentionally inflict severe injuries upon a Police Officer it should be an automatic 20 years in prison. I believe if we continue on the path that we are on, there will be no Law Enforcement Officers, as we know them, in 30-40 years. What happens then?

Enrollment in Law Enforcement Academies is at an all-time low. Law Enforcement job openings are skyrocketing. Police and Sheriff Departments around the country are scrambling in an effort to fill the ever increasing number of open positions, trying to keep their streets and neighborhoods protected.

I can honestly tell you this, if I were just starting out again after high school or college, there is no way on earth I would choose to be a cop, not in the anti-police culture that has been allowed to grow unencumbered for the last few years. There is no such thing as respect for the law anymore, it doesn't exist, because the last generation has taught their children to hate and fear all cops. They are teaching children that the police are dangerous and not to be trusted.

On top of the hatred of Police Officers, we have the courts systematically taking away every tool that is needed by law enforcement in order to do their jobs. The American people need to wake up and realize something. If they want to be safe, secure, and protected, they are going to have to give up a small amount of their right to privacy. It's that simple.

I am not talking about letting "Big Brother" spy on you while you dance around in your wife's bra listening to Alanis Morrissett, but having access, through legal means, to certain information is a critical factor in solving crimes. It baffles the mind that people will jump at the chance to let the giant internet companies have full access to every detail of their lives, but lose their minds the instant the police start asking them questions.

There is no possible way for any law enforcement agency to successfully investigate crimes, identify criminals, trace, locate and return stolen property, solve violent cases, such as Homicide, Rape, and Aggravated Assault, if they are not given the tools to be able to locate people, to track where someone has been and when they were there, to get inside stash houses, drug dens, and vehicles where criminals hide the goods and tools of their trade. It simply cannot happen if a person's "right to privacy" is guaranteed to such a level that law enforcement has absolutely no legal way to access information about that person through the proper channels.

I am by no means a scholar, or expert in social studies, but it doesn't take a lot of education to look around and see what is happening. And small towns like Kaufman, Texas are not immune to the problems that are caused when the government ties the hands of law enforcement; we have the same issues and concerns. The only difference is that we have been lucky not to have had a controversial issue come up………. not yet anyway.

Final Thoughts

One question that is asked of every police applicant is "Why do you want to be a cop?" It's no longer a relevant question. The most common answer, "Because I want to help people", has become a running joke among interviewers. Everyone on an Oral Review Board gets together before the interview and places bets on which applicant will say those words. This happens at every department, large and small. But the absolute truth is, there are only two answers to the question.

There are only two reasons a person becomes a law enforcement officer:

They want to help people who cannot help themselves; or
They want the power and authority that comes with the badge.

There simply are no other honest answers to the question. The latter are the ones that are the most visible. They are the ones that you see on the 5 o'clock news all over the country violating the rights of citizens, beating on people, or killing the person who is running away from them who doesn't have a weapon and is no threat to them or anyone else. It's the true heroes that you never see or hear about, the ones that we should be talking about the most.

My reason for becoming a cop, and staying one for over 20 years, is because I *did want to help people*. It did, and still does, make me feel good when I am able to help or protect someone who isn't able to do it themselves. I *love* to stand between a bully and his victim! There is just no better feeling on earth.

Now, don't get me wrong, I have had my ass beat several times over the years. Some old boys, and girls, were simply bigger, stronger, or on better drugs than I was and were hard to handle. But in every single fight I've been in, the dirt bag went to jail. Sometimes he was bleeding, sometimes I was, but in the end, I won every time. I had to.

Being a cop is the most thankless career on the planet. You get your ass chewed out for doing your job and for not doing your job. Anytime you are doing anything, there are those that complain about you. You are ridiculed for taking a lunch break, for grabbing a cup of coffee or a Dr. Pepper, for stopping and talking to another officer for 5 minutes, for writing a ticket, for not writing a ticket. The list is never ending.

As a cop you see the most disgusting and disturbing things that mankind has to offer. You deal with the worst of humanity, over and over again. There are things I have seen that I hope and pray my children never have to see, people that they never have to come face to face with. It is my hope that I have put away many of the threats that they would have had to face in life.

My career in law enforcement has made me a very cynical person, I know this. I would give anything to be able to change it, but it's just not possible. I have been through too much, seen too much, and been screwed over too many times for it to ever change. I'm not putting on a pity show, I'm simply stating what 20 years of abuse; mental, physical, and financial, has done to me. What it has done to many other men and women that have worn the badge.

There are those people that will say "Well you could have quit at any time". To those of you who think this way, I have this simple message..... Go fuck off. People who say stupid shit like that have no clue what is inside a cop's heart and soul and have never dedicated their life to anything more than ridiculing other people.

So, the question that seems to get asked a lot is; "Would you do it all over again?" For me the answer is a well thought out "No". This career has cost me too much to justify doing it again. I would do something else that allowed me to help those that need it, but no; I would not be a cop again if I could start over. That's just how I feel.

The best thing that a career as a cop gives you is the stories to tell. Stories like the ones I have shared with you in this book. Funny stories, sad stories, disgusting stories, true stories, and some not so true (although every story in this book is absolutely true). Being a cop is never having the exact same day twice. There is always something different from the day before waiting for you when you check on duty. You must always be ready to go from being bored out of your mind, to being in a 100 mph pursuit in a matter of seconds, day in and day out. You must also be ready to deal with the everyday lives of people. That's usually where the best stories come from.

I have made many friends during my time in Kaufman; I've also lost a lot of them. Those that I have known the longest, people like Robin Smith, Lynette and Tommy Bohn, Les Edwards, and Sharna Ellis are the ones that I hope get the most laughs out of this attempt at a book. For the most part they understand me..........I think.

There are stories in this book that most of my family, including my wife, parents, brothers, and my oldest daughter Chelsea, will be hearing for the first time ever. I hope they understand why and don't hold it against me. I never wanted Chelsea to know that her daddy had a dangerous job. She's 25 years old now so I guess I can let the cat out of the bag. *I love you "Buddlebutt"!*

I have described a few fights and struggles that I have experienced, but I haven't told you about the biggest fight of my life. One of the hardest battles I've ever fought was not with a man or woman, but with myself. In early 2007 I was diagnosed with "Major Depressive Disorder", more commonly known as Clinical Depression. This was hard for me to believe, or understand, at first, but the more I read about it, the more I was looking at a portrait of myself painted in the words. My doctor has been with me since that day, helping me understand what was going on with this disease and how it was affecting me. It is something that I will struggle with for the rest of my life and I have accepted it, but I also vowed to fight it every step of the way.

If it wasn't for my beautiful and amazing wife Leslie, things would be so much harder for me. She seems to know exactly how to handle me when things get a little off course, and she will never know how much that means to me. She and my three babies are what keep me going every single day.

As I am getting closer to the end of my career, I find myself still searching for the answers to questions that I've had since the beginning.
Questions like:
- Why do people hurt one another just because their shirt is a different color?

- Why are kids so disrespectful to their parents who sacrifice everything for them?
- What makes someone light a plant on fire and suck it into their bodies?
- And, why don't people understand what cops have to deal with?

I also find myself seeking the answers to newer questions that have come up in my career more recently.
Questions like:
- What makes these young kids, who are just coming out of police academies, think that they automatically deserve respect from the older Officers? We earned our damned respect, now you go earn yours.
- What makes a woman look at a man with tattoos all over his face, head, and neck and decide that he would make a great father for her children?
- Why is that same woman so surprised when her "baby daddy" can't keep a job and provide for her and his kids?
- How is it possible that a kid can stay alive for 18 years on this earth and still be so damned stupid that he robs a store and tries to outrun the cops with his pants down around his knees? *Plan ahead dumbass!*
- Why do women like to wear their pajamas to Walmart?
- Who the hell told all of these yuppies that they would look good with a beard?
- And, how did we, as intelligent American people, ever put ourselves into a position where we had to choose between Hillary Clinton and Donald Trump to be our President? *We screwed the damn pooch on that one!*

I want to thank the citizens of Kaufman, Texas for allowing me to be a part of their lives over the last two decades. Some have enjoyed me being a part of their life a little more than others, but I thank them all just the same. As I have stated before, there have been good times and bad during the last 20 years here at Kaufman PD, but throughout it all, it has definitely been fun!

Me at my desk in the old building in 2012

www.ingramcontent.com/pod-product-compliance
Lightning Source LLC
Chambersburg PA
CBHW051758040426
42446CB00007B/431